THE MEANING OF HISTORY

THE MEANING OF HISTORY

Ronald H. Nash

Broadman & Holman Publishers

Nashville, Tennessee

Printed in the United States of America
0–8054–1400–2
Published by Broadman & Holman Publishers, Nashville, Tennessee

Acquisitions & Development Editor: Leonard G. Goss
Page Design and Typography: TF Designs, Mt. Juliet, Tennessee

Dewey Decimal Classification: 901
Subject Heading: History - Philosophy
Library of Congress Card Catalog Number: 98–12226

Library of Congress Cataloging-in-Publication Data

Nash, Ronald H.
The meaning of history / by Ronald H. Nash
p. cm.
Includes bibliographical references and index.
ISBN 0–8054–1400–2
1. History—Philosophy. I. Title.
D16.8.N34 1998
901—dc21

98–12226
CIP

Some Other Books by Ronald Nash

Faith and Reason: The Search for a Rational Faith

Worldviews in Conflict

The Concept of God

Is Jesus the Only Savior?

When a Baby Dies: The Question of Infant Salvation

Why the Left is Not Right: The Religious Left

Choosing a College

The Word of God and the Mind of Man

Freedom, Justice and the State

The Closing of the American Heart: What's Really Wrong with America's Schools

Poverty and Wealth

The Gospel and the Greeks

The Light of the Mind: St. Augustine's Theory of Knowledge

Christian Faith and Historical Understanding

CONTENTS

PREFACE

This book covers human speculation about the meaning, purpose, and pattern of history from the period of the ancient Greeks through the twentieth-century writings of Oswald Spengler and Arnold Toynbee. It differs from other works in this area, many of them now out-of-print, in the attention it gives to the pattern of history that appears in the Judeo-Christian Scriptures and that was then developed in St. Augustine's fifth-century classic, *The City of God.* The chapters that explore the theories of secular or at least non-Christian theories of history contain a running dialogue between a proponent of the Christian position and the secular positions.

The idea for this book first grew out of a series of courses I began to teach at a large state university more than thirty years ago. I have maintained a keen interest in these matters ever since.

I have written this book for two classes of readers. The first includes students in college and seminary courses that include the material in this work. Such courses are widely taught in departments of history, philosophy, and religion. The second group includes general readers outside of the usual classroom setting who want to know more about the meaning of history and related questions.

This book is a good place for beginners to start their study and for slightly advanced students of the subject to check their previously acquired opinions. Bibliographies at the end of each chapter direct the reader to excellent sources that support more detailed work.

I want to express my thanks for the help received from Scott Armstrong, my student assistant at Reformed Theological Seminary. I also greatly appreciate the assistance provided by Dan Wright, Technical Services Librarian of Reformed Theological Seminary in Orlando, Florida. The quotations from *A Christian View of Men and Things*, by Gordon H. Clark, appear with the permission of The Trinity Foundation.

INTRODUCTION

I wrote this book with at least ten objectives in mind.

(1) I provide the reader with an overview or survey of the field of study known as the philosophy of history or speculative history.

(2) My book examines the ways in which competing world-views or conceptual systems affect both the development and assessment of philosophies of history. No one should be naive enough to think that philosophies of history, or indeed, philosophies of *anything*, are or can be neutral with regard to the religious and moral concerns of the persons who develop such systems.

(3) I show the reader the astounding similarity that existed among the pre-Christian views of history. I refer here to the fact that whether it is ancient Chinese, Indian, Babylonian, Greek, or Roman approaches to history that are in view, all saw history as proceeding in a cyclical pattern.

(4) Many books on this subject acknowledge how the Christian philosophy of history came to influence later secular theories from about A.D. 1700 to the present. This influence can even be found in Karl Marx. Obviously, then, my book will have a great deal to

say about this subject, even when my emphasis at various points takes a different path than some of the other published accounts.

(5) Other books on this subject trace the origins of the Christian philosophy of history back to the writings of St. Augustine (died A.D. 430). While I devote an entire chapter to Augustine's work in this field, I argue that the basic elements of the Christian approach to history appear first in the Old Testament and then appear in the New Testament book authored by the person I call "the first Christian philosopher." I identify that New Testament writer in chapter 5.

(6) My sixth objective is, not surprisingly, to provide an explanation and evaluation of the content of the major approaches to history offered by such individuals as Vico, Kant, Herder, Hegel, Marx, Spengler, and Toynbee.

(7) I also provide the reader with an account of how these later systems "stack up" against the Christian approach to history. I would like to think that readers who heretofore have tended to belittle Christian thinking in such matters might close this book with a significantly higher degree of respect for the Christian tradition. Or, if nothing else, they will recognize that their favorite secular system suffers from serious intellectual flaws.

(8) My chapter on Hegel takes issue with what has become a widely held myth about Hegel's system in general and his view of history in particular. People who left college believing the myth that the key to understanding Hegel is some kind of three-step waltz involving a thesis, antithesis, and synthesis will find that claim challenged in this book. In the process of exploring this issue in relation to Hegel's philosophy of history, I point out what for many is a different way of thinking about Hegel's larger system.

(9) Just as contemporary understanding of Hegel has been compromised by several myths, so too has the thinking of Karl Marx. It has been quite common to find contemporary "interpreters" ignoring the classic Marx under the pretense that one or more readings of Marx devised after 1930 oblige scholars to ignore the interpretations that dominated Western discussions of Marx for almost a full century following the publication of *The Communist Manifesto* in 1848. I argue that the newer interpretations of Marx

need a far more critical reading than Neo-Marxian ideologues seem capable of providing.

(10) The last of my objectives is the desire to explain the serious implications of the newer views of Marx for history as well as for our civilization. Many proponents of newer versions of Marx are hostile to what "history" has traditionally been taken to mean. Many hold opinions in which their view of history becomes effectively indistinguishable from propaganda.

On the Other Hand . . .

While the ten stated objectives of this book may seem rather somber and serious stuff, there are other ways to approach it. I would like to think that many readers will enjoy this material. After all, questions about the meaning, purpose, and pattern of history have for several centuries interested large numbers of the intellectually curious.

Think about readers of this book who might identify themselves as Christians. It is natural for them to think along the following lines: Since I'm a Christian, what does my faith teach about the meaning, purpose, and pattern of history? And how does that teaching differ from the opinions of such famous thinkers as Immanuel Kant, G. W. F. Hegel, and Karl Marx? Is it possible that my Christian beliefs on these matters can compete successfully in the arena of ideas? What really is the meaning and purpose of human history and of my own individual life? Is there a pattern to history? Does history repeat itself in some sense or other? Is history going somewhere? Is it moving toward some concrete and specific event that will prove momentous in the lives of every human who has ever lived? Will there be an end to history? Will that end assume the form of a final, divine judgment? Could there be very many conscious, reflective people uninterested in pursuing the answers to such questions?

I hope readers will find this book interesting and challenging. For those who want to disagree with me or dig more deeply into the material, I provide information about dozens of other books where that digging can be done.

CHAPTER ONE

The Meaning of History

Two quite different approaches to history exist. The first is what some call scientific history. Gordon Graham defines it as "the attempt simply to arrive at an accurate account of past events based upon sufficient evidence, without regard to learning lessons, predicting the future course of events, or grasping the 'meaning' of human history as a whole."[1] This notion of scientific history is all that the word *History* means to many people. It is also what most modern historians focus on in their work. Scientific history seeks knowledge for its own sake, without attention to the practical value of the subject or lessons we might learn from the past or help it might provide with regard to the future.

Gordon Graham defines the second approach to history as the attempt to grasp "the meaning of human history as a whole . . . to look beneath the surface of events and find their inner or ultimate significance."[2] Two names for this approach are *speculative history* and *the philosophy of history*.[3] The best known examples of speculative history are religious in nature, Christianity being an obvious example. *The Meaning of History* is going to deal primarily with this second approach to history.

It would be wrong to think that scientific history and speculative history are totally independent. Philosophers and theologians of history dare not ignore the information about the past supplied by scientific history or the rules that govern scientific research.

The difference between scientific and speculative history is similar to the familiar distinction between seeing some trees and seeing a forest; the philosopher of history attempts to see the larger picture.[4] Whenever we want to go beyond the individual pieces of the puzzle and see the whole picture, we need the help of the philosopher or theologian of history. Such thinkers have wrestled with some or all of the following questions.[5]

(1) *What is the pattern of history?* Several major answers have been offered. St. Augustine and Immanuel Kant, among others, have proposed a *linear* pattern where history has a goal or end toward which it is moving. Others, like the ancient Stoics, have advanced a *cyclical* theory of history; in this view, history supposedly repeats itself in one or more ways. Others, like Vico and Toynbee, combined the linear and cyclical views and offered what has been called a *spiral* theory of history. In their views, while there is a certain repetition in history, there is also progress toward some goal. Finally, a few thinkers have advanced what might be called a *chaotic* view of history. In this view, history has no pattern or meaning.

(2) *What is the mechanism of history?* Speculative philosophers of history have not been content simply to offer patterns of history; they have also attempted to explain how changes in history take place. Among the interesting theories that have been proposed are Hegel's World Hero, Vico's Divine Providence, Marx's Economic Determinism, Toynbee's formula of Challenge and Response, and Spengler's suggestion that each culture follows a determined biological course of birth, growth, and decay.

(3) *What is the purpose or value of history?* The more recent volumes of Arnold Toynbee's *A Study of History* illustrate but one answer to this question: For Toynbee, the end of history is the attainment of a universal religion that justifies and explains the past.

Philosophers of history want to know if history has meaning or whether it is simply "a tale told by an idiot, full of sound and fury, signifying nothing." They also want to know if there is an end or goal toward which history ultimately is moving. Eventually, it becomes relevant to ask where speculative philosophers of history get their pattern. Some thinkers considered in this book claim to get their pattern exclusively from an empirical investigation of history itself. But none of these proposed patterns of history comes from history alone. Some philosophers also offer predictions about the future. Eventually, we will have to ask what grounds are offered in support of such predictions.

John Newport offers a helpful summary of the issues that interest philosophers of history: "What is the ultimate significance of history? Is history merely the result of chance or inexorable Fate, or is it a divine drama with a plot, a plan, or a goal? Is there a hidden master Dramatist? These questions are significant and vitally related to human life and destiny, to our highest hopes and deepest fears. For if there is no purpose, how can we do anything but despair?"[6]

The Importance of Speculative History

There are times when we need something more than scientific history. This is especially true during times of great crisis. Imagine a soldier the night before entering combat. As he lies in the dark, unable to sleep, can he help but wonder what is happening on the larger scale of history at that moment? What will happen tomorrow? Will he live or die? And whatever happens to him, will the events of the next day play some role in a larger purpose? During times of crisis, people understandably want to know what is happening and why. When peace and security seem to be disappearing before our very eyes, it is natural to wonder if our lives and the history of which we are a part have any meaning.

Speculative history is also important because human beings want and need more than the detached perspective of the scientific historian.[7] Just as we seek the meaning of events in our own lives, we also welcome a perspective that will help us understand the destiny of the whole human race. Beliefs about the meaning of history can have a significant impact upon our understanding of ourselves, of other people, and of nations and entire civilizations.

Because there are so many conflicting patterns of history, so many opposing answers about the meaning, purpose, and goal of history, we need information about the options that are out there so we can make intelligent choices. Speculative history is also important because of the role such theories have played in shaping dangerous ideologies. The horrible deeds committed by German fascists and by communists from many nations were one consequence of their views of history. People committed themselves to such ideologies believing that they were ways of changing history and the world "for the better." At the present time, new ideologies, with their own views of history, threaten important human values. These ideologies can be found in nations such as North Korea, Iran, and Iraq. How can people who oppose such positions provide an alternative when they are unable to articulate and defend their own worldview, including their philosophy of history? It is easy to suppose that one reason why many Christians do such a bad job of relating the Christian view of history is because they themselves understand so little about speculative history. This book may be helpful in countering this problem.

Scientific History and the Christian Faith

Scientific history is important to Christianity because it teaches that God has revealed himself in history. Historian Herbert Butterfield explains that Christianity is a historical religion because "it presents us with religious doctrines which are at the same time historical events or historical interpretations."[8] Moreover, Butterfield adds, "Certain historical events are held to be part of the [Christian] religion itself—they are considered to have a spiritual content and to represent the divine breaking in upon history."[9] Christians believe that in Jesus Christ, God actually entered into human history.

Christianity is also a historical religion in the sense that the occurrences of certain events, like the Crucifixion and the Resurrection of Jesus of Nazareth, are necessary conditions for its truth. If such an event as the Resurrection of Christ can be shown to have happened in history, important Christian claims will be vindicated. Some Christian thinkers go so far as to claim that historical evidence can actually "prove"[10] or provide warrant for the truth of many Christian beliefs. While others insist that the evidence falls short of definitive proof, they agree that history can provide evidence that strengthens the plausibility of the Christian faith.

Some whose beliefs are antithetical to Christianity get equally excited about the possibility that historical evidence might falsify essential Christian beliefs. British theologian T. A. Roberts is correct when he states that "the truth of Christianity is anchored in history; hence the implicit recognition that if some or all of the events upon which Christianity has traditionally thought to be based could be proved unhistorical, then the religious claims of Christianity would be seriously jeopardized."[11]

Students of the New Testament know that the apostle Paul acknowledged the inseparable link between historical reality and Christian faith; if Christ did not rise from the dead in the way described in the gospels, Paul writes that "our preaching is useless and so is your faith" (1 Cor. 15:14). Paul's dramatic conversion from an enemy of the Christian faith to a leader of the early Christian church was grounded upon his own personal encounter with the risen Christ.[12] The Christian faith deserves credit for the central place it gives to history, certainly more than many of its critics will admit. Many religious traditions typically float in a historical never-never land, immune from any threat that might follow from historical inaccuracies or, for that matter, the absence of any link to historical events in the world of space and time. For those who understand the important link between history and faith, this is hardly something that enhances the plausibility of those traditions in the world of ideas.

Christianity and Speculative History

Christianity attaches great significance both to scientific and speculative history. Such events as the birth, death, and resurrection of Jesus Christ are important because they provide the Christian faith with the key to unlocking the importance and meaning of the historical process. As Gordon H. Clark points out:

> It could hardly be otherwise. If the second person of the Triune God actually became flesh and dwelt amongst us, and died on the cross for men, that event would naturally overshadow every other aspect of the world, scientific or historical. And such a descent of Deity into human affairs would not only involve a theory of history logically, but must psychologically provoke some general reflection on history. Both logically and actually therefore Christianity has a philosophy of history.[13]

According to British scholar Christopher Dawson:

> The Christian interpretation of history is inseparable from the Christian faith. It is not a philosophic theory which has been elaborated by the intellectual effort of Christian scholars. It is an integral part of the Christian revelation; indeed that revelation is essentially an historic one, so that the most metaphysical of its dogmas are based upon historic facts and form part of that great dispensation of grace in which the whole temporal process of the life of humanity finds its end and meaning.[14]

And so the Christian faith contains a philosophy of history.

But which version of Christianity are we talking about, since there are many denominations and theologies to choose from? Many decades ago, theologian J. Gresham Machen offered a historical test of the nature of Christianity. Since Christianity "is an historical phenomenon like the state of Pennsylvania or the U.S.A.," Machen argued, "it must be investigated by historical means."[15] He then asked what point in Christianity's long history should be investigated to discover its true nature. His answer was that we should turn to the beginning of the faith.

The proper way to discover the nature of Christianity is to go back to *its* original document, the New Testament Scriptures. Machen's point was that the early founders of Christianity had a right to legislate the essential nature of Christianity for all subsequent generations choosing to bear the name "Christian." He argued that if we change their beliefs, we should have the honesty to change the name. "It is misleading to use the old name to designate a new thing."[16]

This, however, is the very thing that many varieties of theology in Christendom refuse to acknowledge, promoting the idea that the word *Christianity* should mean whatever "Christians" today believe and do. This creates enormous confusion by opening the door to pagan beliefs and practices.[17]

But what about the obvious fact that people calling themselves Christians disagree over how to interpret the Bible? The way to deal with this problem is found in the path Christians down through history have followed: Master the original languages, formulate proper hermeneutical methods, get into the text, examine the historical and literary context, and then evaluate conflicting interpretations. If nothing else, this takes us beyond the subjectivity and relativism that is the legacy of many forms of modern theology.

Since the ultimate authority for Christians is (or ought to be) the Christian Scriptures, a necessary task for Christians concerned about history is to systematize from the content of Scripture the most important things it has to say about history. Is there a Christian pattern of history? If so, what is it? What is the Christian account of the mechanism of history and the value and purpose of history? What is the Christian answer to questions about the meaning of history? Where does the Christian pattern of history come from? And since we know the Christian Scriptures make predictions about the future, what are the grounds of those predictions?

What Comes Next?

Before I begin my analysis and evaluation of what I regard as the most important systems of speculative history, it is important to lay a foundation for this task through a study of the important and necessary role that worldviews play in any approach to questions about the meaning of history. We will not get far in our investigation of philosophies of history if we ignore the intellectual and personal biases that are often carried into this field. This is the subject to which I now turn.

CHAPTER TWO

WORLDVIEWS AND THE MEANING OF HISTORY

One of the more important things to do before undertaking a search for the meaning of history is to examine how worldview thinking influences the way people approach such a subject. If one is serious about getting somewhere in an examination of competing theories of history, it is necessary to examine the bigger picture, in this case, the worldviews of which theories of history are but a part. People committed to different worldviews typically find it difficult to appreciate the perspectives that shape the thinking and conduct of others. Obviously, such comments apply to the issues that arise in a search for the meaning of history.

A worldview or conceptual framework is that pattern of concepts (ideas) by which people organize their beliefs and that enables them to make sense of the world. This framework or worldview is a comprehensive and systematic view of life and of the world. Just as surely as Plato and Aristotle had a worldview, so too does each reader of this book, along with every person who has ever sought to think reflectively about history. Consciously or unconsciously, our worldviews affect the way we interpret and judge reality, and they inevitably influence what we believe and how we live. No one has a choice regarding whether they will have a worldview. Rather, the choice concerns what kind of worldview we will adopt and how it will affect our understanding of history.

What Is a Worldview?

Many people have no idea what a worldview is. Many are unaware of the specific content of their personal worldview, or even that they have one. Worldviews function much like eyeglasses. When people look at the world through the wrong conceptual system, it doesn't make much sense to them. It is also true that what they think makes sense will often be wrong. Putting on the right conceptual scheme, that is, viewing the world through the correct worldview, can have important consequences for the rest of a person's thinking and acting.

Most of us know people who seem incapable of seeing certain points that are obvious to us; perhaps they view us as equally obtuse or stubborn. They often seem to have some built-in grid that filters out information and arguments and that leads them to place some peculiar twist on things in ways that we find hard to understand. Such behavior is often a result of their worldview. The inability of some people to be open to new beliefs, or to think critically about their own beliefs is often a function of the conceptual system that influences or even determines the way they approach the world and the claims of others. Many disagreements between individuals, societies, and entire nations are often actually clashes of competing worldviews. As we will see, this is certainly true regarding disputes over the meaning of history. It should be obvious that one of the more important tasks for a philosopher is to help people realize what a worldview is, assist them in achieving a better understanding of their own worldview, and then equip them to improve upon their worldview by filling in gaps and removing inconsistencies where these exist.

There are several reasons to use classical Christian theism as an example of a worldview. Many people, including large numbers who consider themselves Christian, fail to understand that Christianity is a consistent world-and-life view. Moreover, many people misunderstand important features of the Christian perspective. Finally, a proper grasp of the Christian worldview will make it much easier to understand the Christian approach to history that plays such an important role in this book.

The Framework of Christian Theism

Many people mistakenly think of Christian theism as a collection of unrelated beliefs and claims. But the Christian faith should be approached as a conceptual system, as a total world-and-life view. Once it is understood that both Christianity and its adversaries in the world of ideas are in fact full-blown worldviews, we are in a better position to judge the relative merits of rival systems.

Worldviews contain at least six clusters of beliefs about God, ultimate reality, knowledge, morality, human nature, and history. They may include other important beliefs, but these need not concern us here. These six are usually the ones that define the most important differences among competing conceptual systems. Spatial limitations permit us to cover only some of the more essential elements of the Christian worldview.

God

The Christian world-and-life perspective teaches the existence of one supremely powerful and personal God. This position, known as Theism, differs from polytheism (belief in many gods), pantheism (belief in an impersonal deity who is somehow identical with the world), and panentheism (believing that God and the world are co-eternal and co-dependent parts of the same ultimate reality).[1] Other important attributes of God, such as his omnipotence, omniscience, holiness, justice, and love, are affirmed in Scripture and thus constitute vital elements of the Christian worldview's account of God.[2]

Historical Christian theism is also trinitarian. The doctrine of the Trinity reflects the Christian conviction that the Father, the Son, and the Holy Spirit are three distinct centers of consciousness sharing fully in the one divine nature and in the activities of the other persons of the Trinity. God is Father, Son, and Holy Spirit.

Each of these is distinct from the others, and yet there is only one God. An important corollary of this doctrine is the Christian conviction that Jesus Christ is both fully God and fully man.[3]

Ultimate Reality

The Christian worldview teaches that God created *ex nihilo*[4] everything that exists. This belief is endemic to Christianity, inasmuch as any denial of the doctrine leads logically to severe constraints upon the power and sovereignty of God. Such a competing view of God would effectively produce a different and opposing worldview; it could not be Christian in the historic sense of the word. A God powerful enough to create the universe and the laws by which it operates can hardly have problems controlling the universe in ways that make possible such extraordinary events as miracles, prophecy, and providence.

In the historic[5] Christian understanding of things, the existence of the world is not a brute fact, nor is the world a purposeless machine. The doctrine of creation implies that the world God created is real. This contrasts with some Asian worldviews that regard all of reality as an illusion. The reality of the world means that there is something here for us to investigate and know. The doctrine of creation also implies that the world is intelligible, that it can be known. Finally, it implies that God's creation is good. The Christian worldview disagrees with other systems that view the world as illusory or unintelligible.

Knowledge

A third belief that characterizes Christianity teaches that the personal, sovereign, all-knowing triune God can reveal true propositions to the human mind and that this divine special revelation is an indispensable and legitimate source of information.[6] Since the Christian worldview is no ally of skepticism, it obviously has much to say about human knowledge.[7] Human beings can know God's creation; they can also attain knowledge about God and his actions in history.

It would be foolish to separate the Christian God from his self-disclosure in the Bible. Such a separation would amount to a renunciation of an essential element of the Christian worldview.[8]

It misrepresents the Christian position to suggest that the Bible only enters the Christian worldview through some kind of irrational, blind "leap of faith."

Morality

Another essential tenet of the Christian worldview is the fact that all human beings carry the image of God. This explains why we are capable of love, God-consciousness, and reasoning; it also explains why we are moral creatures. Sin (yet another essential Christian tenet) has distorted the image of God and explains why humans turn away from God and his moral law. Because we carry God's image, we should expect to find that the ethical principles of the Christian worldview reflect what all of us at the deepest level of our moral being know to be true.

According to the Christian worldview, God is the basis of the laws that govern the physical universe and that make possible the order of the cosmos. God is also the basis of the moral laws that ought to govern human behavior and that make social order possible. Christian theism insists on the existence of universal moral laws that apply to all, regardless of when or where humans have lived. These moral laws are objective in the sense that their truth is independent of human preference and desire.

Human Nature

Human beings are more than physical beings. No system that reduces humans to the lowest common material denominator, that denies the wonder and glory of the human mind, that rejects the possibility of redemption from sin and eternal life, can be consistent with the worldview that Christians draw from God's revealed truth in Scripture. The Christian worldview also teaches that every human being is born with a nature inclined toward sin. Christianity is opposed to systems teaching that people are inherently good, or that their evil acts are simply a result of bad education or environment.

History

During the early centuries of the Christian church, many competing religious systems in the Mediterranean world belittled the importance of history. For example, the various ancient worldviews often referred to as "mystery religions" had no essential connection with the real world of space and time. Followers of those religions would never have changed their religious beliefs and practices had someone convinced them that the myths and legends so central to their worldviews had no link to history.[9] This is also true of the major Asian religions, such as Buddhism, Hinduism, and Shintoism. But it is not true of the Christian faith.

As already explained, Christianity has always had a special interest in history. Not only does Christianity teach that God is Lord over history (in the sense that history began in his act of creation, is governed by his providence, and will end at his judgment), it also holds that through Christ, God actually entered into human history. In an important sense, Christianity is grounded upon certain revelatory events (such as the Crucifixion and the Resurrection) that took place in the real world of space and time.

Summary

Christianity is a conceptual system, a worldview. Once people understand that both Christian theism and other religious and philosophical systems in the world of ideas are worldviews, they will be in a better position to judge the strengths and weaknesses of the total Christian system. The case for or against Christian theism should be made and evaluated in terms of all the important things it has to say about the whole of human life. Many reject Christianity not because of their problems with one or two isolated issues, but because their anti-Christian conceptual scheme leads them to reject information and arguments that for believers provide support for the Christian faith claim.

Every worldview has questions it appears to answer unsatisfactorily. One task of Christian intellectual activity is to show that none of the problems attributed to Christian theism provides sufficient reasons for rational people to reject it.

A Competing Worldview

Many readers who are new to worldview thinking might encounter some difficulty getting the whole picture from just one example. It will help to provide one more example of a worldview, this time one that is almost the complete opposite of the Christian system.

The major competition to the Christian worldview in the West has been[10] a system that often goes by the name of Naturalism. The basic presupposition of Metaphysical Naturalism[11] states that nothing exists outside the material, mechanical (that is, nonpurposeful), natural order. Philosopher William Halverson unpacks some of the details of this thought system:

> Naturalism asserts, first of all, that the primary constituents of reality are material entities. By this I do not mean that only material entities exist; I am not denying the reality—the real existence—of such things as hopes, plans, behavior, language, logical inferences, and so on. What I am asserting, however, is that anything that is real is, in the last analysis, explicable as a material entity or as a form or function or action of a material entity.[12]

What about God and the notion of creation? Halverson explains: "Theism says, 'In the beginning, God'; naturalism says, 'In the beginning, matter.'"[13]

Naturalism teaches that the universe is a closed system in the sense that everything that happens within the universe is caused by or explained by other natural events "within the system." Hence, there is never a need to seek the explanation of anything that exists in some alleged reality that lies "outside" the natural order. Nature then can be viewed as a type of closed box. Everything that happens inside the box (the natural order) is caused by or is explained in terms of other things that exist within the box. Nothing (including God) exists outside the box; therefore, nothing outside the box that we call the universe or nature can have any causal effect within the box. The resulting picture of naturalism looks like this:

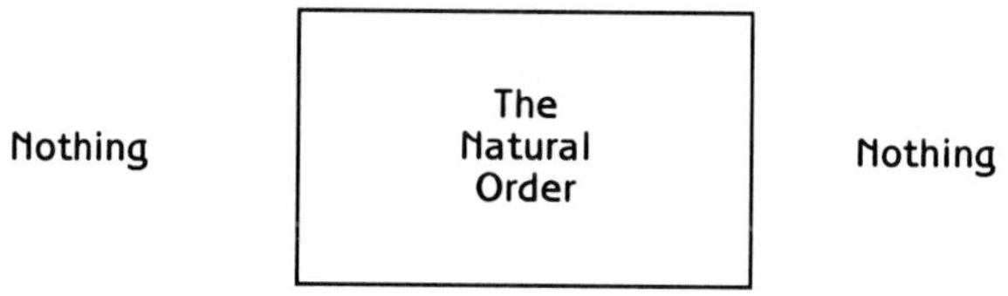

Nothing | The Natural Order | Nothing

Given these presuppositions it is small wonder that those influenced by Naturalism object to major elements of the Christian worldview. Believers in Naturalism are precluded from believing in God, spirit, soul, angels, miracles, prophecy, prayer, providence, immortality, heaven, sin, and salvation as Christians normally understand these notions for one simple reason: Such beliefs are logically incompatible with the naturalist's worldview.

A metaphysical naturalist, then, is someone who believes the following propositions:

1. Only nature exists
2. Nature is a materialistic system
3. Nature is a self-explanatory system
4. Nature is characterized by total uniformity
5. Nature is a deterministic system

Clearly, any persons in the grip of these naturalistic habits of mind will be unable to believe in the kinds of miracles described in the Bible; it would be inconsistent for them to do so. Once one's worldview precludes miracles, it becomes logically impossible for such a person to believe in the historic Christian faith. Naturalists cannot be true to their worldview and believe in special revelation, prophecy, providence, and other forms of divine control over reality. Thus, no arguments on behalf of the Christian perspective can possibly succeed against Naturalism on *Naturalism's* own terms. The only proper way to address the naturalists' disbelief is to *begin* by challenging the elements of their naturalism.

Naturalism and Theism Contrasted

In what important ways does Christian theism differ from Naturalism? The following figure of the Christian worldview is a good place to start.

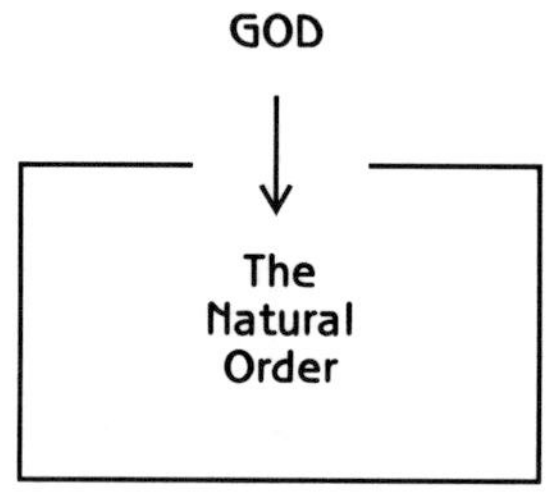

This diagram illustrates three important elements of the Christian worldview:

1. God exists outside the box
2. God created the box
3. God acts causally within the box

Christian theism, then, rejects Naturalism's contention that nothing, including God, exists outside the natural order. It also denies that the natural world of physical objects has always existed. God created the world freely and *ex nihilo*. The universe is contingent in the sense that it could not have begun to exist without God's creative act, and it could not continue to exist without God's sustaining activity.

It is especially important to note that aside from the fact that the box is "open" to causes existing outside the box, the Christian's scientific understanding of the natural order need not differ in any way from that of the naturalist.[14] Christians believe that nature exhibits patterns of order and regularity. Of course, they also believe that this uniformity results from God's free decision to create the universe in a particular way. Christian theism recognizes the same cause-and-effect order within the natural order as does the naturalist. The Christian believes, however, that the natural order depends on God both for its existence and its order. When Christians assert that God is capable of acting causally within the natural order, they do not mean necessarily that such divine action results in a suspension or violation of the natural order.[15] But whether or not miracles are exceptions to the laws of nature, the world is not closed to God's causal activity.

Finally, Christian theism denies that nature is a self-explanatory system. The very existence of the contingent universe requires that we seek the cause of its being in a necessary being, one that does not depend upon anything else for its existence. Laws operating within the natural order owe their existence to God's creative activity. And many things that happen within the natural order are affected by, or influenced by, or brought about by free acts of the personal God.

The Case Against Naturalism

A careful analysis of Naturalism reveals a problem so serious that it fails one of the major tests that rational persons expect any worldview to pass.[16] In order to see how this is so, it is necessary first to recall that Naturalism regards the universe as a self-contained and self-explanatory system. There is nothing outside the box we call nature that can explain, or that is necessary to explain, anything inside the box. Naturalism claims that every existing object or event can be explained in terms of something else within the natural order. This dogma is not an accidental or nonessential feature of the naturalistic position. All that is required for Naturalism to be false is the discovery of one thing that cannot be explained in the naturalistic way.

C. S. Lewis sets up the line of argument I wish to consider:

> If necessities of thought force us to allow to any one thing any degree of independence from the Total System—if any one thing makes good a claim to be on its own, to be something more than an expression of the character of Nature as a whole—then we have abandoned Naturalism. For by Naturalism we mean the doctrine that only Nature—the whole interlocked system—exists. And if that were true, every thing and event would, if we knew enough, be explicable without remainder . . . as a necessary product of the system.[17]

With a little effort, we can quickly see that no thoughtful naturalist can ignore at least one thing that exists "outside the box." Lewis explains:

> All possible knowledge . . . depends on the validity of reasoning. If the feeling of certainty which we express by words like *must be* and *therefore* and *since* is a real perception of how things outside our minds really "must" be, well and good. But if this certainty is merely a feeling *in* our minds and not a genuine insight into realities beyond them—if it merely represents the ways our minds happen to work—then we have no knowledge. Unless human reasoning is valid no science can be true.[18]

And, we might add, unless human reasoning is valid no arguments by any metaphysical naturalist directed against Christian theism or offered in support of Naturalism can be sound.

The human mind, as we know, has the power to grasp contingent truths, that is, things that *are* the case though they might not *have been* the case. But the human mind also has the power to grasp *necessary connections,* that is, what *must* be the case. This latter power, the ability to grasp *necessary* connections, is the hallmark of human *reasoning.* What I am here calling a necessary connection may be illustrated by the following familiar syllogism. If it is true that all men are mortal, and if it is true that Socrates is a man, then it *must* be true that Socrates is mortal. Almost anyone can see, even without special training in logic, that the conclusion, *Socrates is mortal*, must be true if the other two propositions are true.

Naturalists themselves must appeal to this kind of necessary connection in their own arguments for Naturalism. Indeed, they must make this appeal in their reasoning about anything. But can naturalists account for this essential element of the reasoning process that they use in their arguments for their own position? When Naturalism discredits human reasoning, it becomes impossible for naturalists to provide arguments in support of their own position. This is so because no explanation of the universe, including Metaphysical Naturalism,

> can be true unless that account leaves it possible for our thinking to be a real insight. A theory which explained everything else in the whole universe but which made it impossible to believe that our thinking was valid, would be utterly out of court. For that theory would itself have been reached by thinking, and if thinking is not valid that theory would, of course, be itself demolished. It would have destroyed its own credentials. It would be an argument which proved that no argument was sound—a proof that there are no such things as proofs—which is nonsense.[19]

Lewis is careful to point out that his argument is *not* grounded on the claim that Metaphysical Naturalism affirms that every human judgment (like every event in the universe) has a cause. He understands that even though a belief about a matter may be caused by nonrational factors, that belief may still be true.[20] In the argument before us, Lewis is talking about something else, namely, the logical connection between a belief and the ground of that belief. It is one thing for a belief to have a nonrational cause; it is something else for a belief to have a reason or ground. The ravings of a madman may have a cause but lack any justifying ground. The reasoning of a philosopher may also have a cause but possess a justifying ground.[21] What Metaphysical Naturalism does, according to Lewis, is sever what should be unseverable—the necessary connection between conclusions and the grounds or reasons for those conclusions. As Lewis says, "Unless our conclusion is the logical consequent from a ground it will be worthless [as an example of a *reasoned* conclusion] and could be true only by a fluke."[22] Therefore, Naturalism "offers what professes to be a full account of our mental behavior; but this account, on inspection, leaves no room for the acts of knowing or insight on which the whole value of our thinking, as a means to truth, depends."[23]

A Summary

Metaphysical Naturalism necessarily excludes the possible existence of anything beyond nature, outside the box. But the process of reasoning *requires* something that exceeds the bounds of nature, namely, the laws of logical inference. It is difficult to see how Metaphysical Naturalism can show how any instance of human reasoning can ever be valid. As a worldview, Naturalism is incompatible with attitudes of trust in our rational faculties and our ability to attain knowledge about anything, including the possible truth of Naturalism. As Richard Purtill argues, this self-destructive feature of Naturalism is "rather like the man who saws off the branch he is sitting on. The only cold comfort [metaphysical naturalists] hold out is that some of our thoughts might happen to agree with reality."[24] But on naturalistic grounds, we can never know that they do.

One of Naturalism's major problems, then, is explaining how mindless forces give rise to minds, knowledge, sound reasoning, and moral principles that suggest how human beings ought to behave.[25] Not surprisingly, naturalists want the rest of us to think that *their* worldview, *their* Naturalism, is a product of *their* sound reasoning. All things considered, Naturalism is self-referentially absurd. Before any person can justify his or her acceptance of Naturalism on rational grounds, it is first necessary for that person to reject a cardinal tenet of the naturalist position. In other words, the only way a person can provide rational grounds for believing in Naturalism is first to cease being a naturalist.

This self-defeating feature of Naturalism does not prove by itself that theism is true. There are enough other alternatives to Naturalism that the falsity of Naturalism does not entail the truth of theism. Nevertheless, the incoherence of Naturalism certainly enhances the plausibility of its major competitor in the conflict among worldviews, namely, Christian theism.

Much of the opposition to the Christian view of history in the West comes from people controlled by the presuppositions of Naturalism. Naturalists need to recognize the extent to which their beliefs about divine providence, God's plan in history, and the possibility of divine special revelation and miracles are dictated by their naturalistic presuppositions. Opposition to the Christian view of history is not due to naturalists' greater intelligence or enlightenment; it is because of their worldview. Metaphysical naturalists need to reflect on the self-defeating nature of Naturalism and determine whether they can do better in choosing a worldview. In so doing, naturalists have a much better chance of making sense of the Christian worldview and its understanding of history.

Personal Considerations

A disagreement between adherents of two worldviews is to some extent a cognitive matter. That is, it has some relationship to beliefs, truth claims, and arguments. Of course it would be foolish to pretend that we always handle such matters impersonally and objectively, without reference to considerations rooted in our psychological makeup. Many people act in ways that reveal they are incapable of thinking clearly about their worldview. Most of us have met people so captive to some conceptual scheme that they seem incapable of giving a fair hearing to any argument or piece of evidence that threatens their cherished system. This is true of both theists and nontheists.

It is simply true that many people have difficulty accepting certain belief systems because of their philosophical presuppositions. Yet people's theoretical judgments often seem inordinately affected by nontheoretical factors. This is the case, for example, when racial prejudice leads some to hold untrue beliefs about people who are the objects of their prejudice.

Another type of nontheoretical factor may influence our thinking. According to some writers, human beings are never neutral regarding God. Either we worship God as Creator and Lord, or we turn away. Because the human heart (the center or religious root of our being) is directed either toward or against God, theoretical thinking is never as pure or autonomous as many would like to suppose. While this raises questions that cannot be explored further in this book,[26] it seems obvious that some people who appear to reject Christianity on what they regard as rational theoretical grounds are, in fact, acting under the influence of nonrational factors (that is, the more ultimate commitments of their hearts). We should all be encouraged to dig below the surface and uncover the basic philosophical and religious presuppositions that often appear to control our thinking. Each of the conflicting theories of speculative history surveyed in this book provides an opportunity for us to look for nontheoretical and even religious influences at work in our presuppositions.

Though the influence of nontheoretical factors on people's thinking is often extensive, it is seldom total. Even in cases like Saul of Tarsus—one of early Christianity's greatest enemies—where it might appear that a person was totally dominated by commitments that ruled out any possibility of a change or conversion, life-altering changes may occur. People do change conceptual systems. Conversions take place all the time. People who used to be humanists or naturalists or atheists or followers of some competing religious faith have found reasons to turn away from their old conceptual systems and embrace Christianity. Conversely, people who used to profess allegiance to Christianity reach a point where they feel they can no longer believe. In spite of all the obstacles, people do occasionally begin to doubt conceptual systems they have accepted for years.

It is probably not possible to identify a single set of necessary conditions that are always present when people change a worldview. After all, many remain blissfully unaware that they have a worldview, even though a sudden change in life and thought results from exchanging an old worldview for a new one. What does seem clear is that dramatic changes usually require a period of doubt about key elements of the worldview. Even when changes may appear suddenly, in all likelihood they are preceded by a period of growing uncertainty and doubt. In many cases the actual change is triggered by an important event, often a crisis of some kind. But many will recount stories that lay out a different scenario. Suddenly, or so it seemed, one event or piece of information led them to begin thinking along entirely different lines, to accept a conceptual scheme that was totally different for them, or one they were becoming conscious of for the first time. Quite unexpectedly, these people "saw" things they had overlooked before. Suddenly they "saw" things fit together in a pattern so that there was meaning where none had been discernible before. It seems quite foolish, therefore, to stipulate that life-transforming changes in a worldview must match some pattern. People change their minds on important subjects for a bewildering variety of reasons or nonreasons.

The Important Question of Religious Neutrality

I have argued that all who engage in scientific, philosophical, and other forms of intellectual pursuits need to pay more attention to the ways that worldview considerations shape, influence, and in many cases determine our conclusions. I now wish to go further and maintain that all intellectual activities have an inescapable religious component.

Religious faith is not merely an isolated compartment of a person's life that one can take or leave as one wishes. It is rather a dimension of life that colors or influences everything we do and believe. John Calvin taught that all human beings are "incurably religious." Religion is an inescapable given in life. Paul Tillich was right when he defined religion as a matter of "ultimate concern." Religion is more than this, but it cannot be less. We all have something that concerns us ultimately, and whatever it is, that object of ultimate concern is our God. Whatever a person's *ultimate* concern may be, it will have a powerful influence on everything else done or believed.

This view was shared by the late Henry Zylstra who wrote:

> To be human is to be scientific, yes, and practical, and rational, and moral, and social, and artistic, but to be human further is to be religious also. And this religious [dimension] in man is not just another facet of himself, just another side to his nature, just another part of the whole. It is the condition of all the rest and the justification of all the rest. This is inevitably and inescapably so for all men. No man is religiously neutral in his knowledge of and his appropriation of reality.[27]

No one is religiously neutral. Whether an atheistic philosopher offering arguments against the existence of God, or a psychologist attributing belief in God to some cognitive malfunction, or an ACLU lawyer attempting another tactic to remove religion from the public square, no human is religiously neutral. The world is not composed of religious and nonreligious people; it is composed rather of religious people who have differing ultimate concerns, different gods, and who respond to the Living God in different ways. Each human life manifests different ways of expressing our allegiances and our answers to the ultimate questions of life. All humans are incurably religious; we simply manifest *different* religious allegiances.

This point dismisses much of the usual distinction between things sacred and secular. Any philosopher or historian who pretends to be religiously neutral is either suffering from self-deception or is a fraud. Secular Humanism is a *religious* worldview as certainly as Christianity and Judaism. It expresses the ultimate commitments and concerns of its proponents.

But it is now necessary to close the circle. The question of moral and religious values must be broadened to include the larger issues of worldviews. As we have seen, every person has a worldview. These worldviews function like eyeglasses in that they are interpretive conceptual schemes that explain why we "see" the world as we do, and why we think and act as we do. Worldviews are double-edged swords. An inadequate worldview (or conceptual scheme) can, like poorly prescribed eyeglasses, hinder our efforts to understand God, the world, our history, and ourselves. The right conceptual scheme can suddenly bring everything into proper focus.

Just as it is impossible to separate historical reflection from one's worldview, it is equally impossible to divorce reflection about history from one's ultimate concern (religion).

Conclusion

We will continue to encounter worldview questions throughout the rest of this book. Each system of speculative history we examine will reflect the theoretical (worldview) and nontheoretical commitments of its creator. We need to dig down to the foundations of each system to see what the various authors believe about God, ultimate reality, knowledge, morality, human nature, and, of course, the meaning and purpose of history.

We need to understand how one's worldview either helps or hinders the search for the meaning of history. The Christian worldview provides warrant for believing in divine special revelation, miracles, prophecy, prayer, and providence. It grounds our conclusions about the purpose and meaning of history, the eternal significance of individual human persons, and our hope for the future. As we proceed, we must continue to ask whether the worldviews behind the secular systems of history provide an equally adequate ground for their authors' conclusions.

For Further Reading

C. S. Lewis, *Miracles* (New York: Macmillan, 1960).

Ronald Nash, *Faith and Reason* (Grand Rapids: Zondervan, 1988).

Ronald Nash, *Worldviews in Conflict* (Grand Rapids: Zondervan, 1992).

Richard L. Purtill, *Reason to Believe* (Grand Rapids: Eerdmans, 1974).

CHAPTER THREE

The Cyclical View of History

Almost all of the great civilizations existing before the beginning of the Christian era ascribed a cyclical pattern to history. This was true in most of the great ancient cultures, including Babylonia, Persia, ancient Egypt, India, China, Greece, and Rome.[1] I will focus on the cyclical pattern in Greece and Rome.

British author J. B. Bury says that "the theory of world-cycles was so widely current that it may almost be described as the orthodox theory of cosmic time among the Greeks, and it passed from them to the Romans."[2] The cyclical pattern was based no doubt on human observation of such things as the daily recurrence of night and day, the monthly phases of the moon and yearly phases of the sun. In some ancient writers, this cycle was thought to be connected to the time required for the planets to reach a position in the heavens related to some particular date. According to some writers, this period of time was thought to take 36,000 years.[3] It was customary to refer to the wheel or cycle as "the Great Year."

British scholar John Baillie claims a doctrine of eternal recurrence can be found in a number of philosophers before Socrates, including Anaximander, Anaximenes, Heraclitus, Parmenides, and the Pythagoreans. In the case of some Pythagoreans, Bury notes, "each cycle repeated to the minutest particular the course and events of the preceding . . . As no end seems to have been assigned to the whole process, the course of the world's history would contain an endless number of Trojan Wars, for instance; an endless number of Platos would write an endless number of *Republics.*"[4] Baillie draws special attention to references to the Great Year in the writings of both Plato and Aristotle.[5]

Two Forms of Cyclicism

Two different forms of a cyclical pattern appear in this book. The version that will occupy most of our attention in this chapter teaches that the sequence of historical events in the cycle we are living in has repeated itself many times in the past and will continue to be repeated in the future. Later in the book, we will find a different version that restricts cyclicism to the rise and fall of nations and civilizations. In this second theory, history is repetitive but each subsequent repetition is different in important ways. This approach will be found in the twentieth-century writings of Oswald Spengler and Arnold Toynbee. One would have to be quite inattentive not to notice how different nations have become powerful, only to decline into weakness and then fade from view. But it would be unwise to get carried away in such matters and conclude that one has discovered a similiar pattern in the development of different nations. Greece became great and powerful and then fell, as did Rome, the Holy Roman Empire, and the British Empire. But the reasons why these and other nations gained and then lost power differed greatly. It is difficult—some would say impossible—to find anything approximating similar reasons; no generalizations apply to every case. The evaluation of the second form of cyclicism appears in treatment of Spengler and Toynbee in chapter 11.

A Serious Problem

The cyclical theory of history found among the Greeks and Romans depreciated history. If history goes round and round, never getting anywhere, forever repeating itself, there can be no goal either for individual humans or for the species. Whatever happens to humans will happen again; whatever humans accomplish, they must accomplish again and again—forever. It was Christianity that sought to counter the pessimistic view of history found in pagan philosophy with a theory that lent meaning and significance to history. As John Warwick Montgomery explains,

> The importance of the Biblical conception [of history] cannot be overstressed. Here for the first time Western man was presented with a purposive, goal-directed interpretation of history. The Classical doctrine of recurrence had been able to give a "substantiality" to history, but it had not given it any aim or direction. It is not strange that Classical man lost interest in history when it represented to him no more than eternally repetitious events. But for the "people of God" in Israel and in the Church, history was definitely "going somewhere."[6]

There is no better way for a professor to illustrate the despair created by a cyclical approach to history than to remind students that such a view would require them to reread this page an infinite number of times.

Stoicism

The cyclical view of history in Greece and Rome received its most systematic formulation in the school of thought known as Stoicism, which reached its greatest influence between 100 B.C. and A.D. 200.

Stoicism passed through three major stages: (1) The Early Stoa, dated roughly from 300 to 200 B.C., included thinkers active during the beginning of the movement: Zeno of Citium, the founder of the school (336–264 B.C.), Cleanthes (331–232 B.C.), and Chrysippus (280–204 B.C.); (2) The two major representatives of the Middle Stoa—dated approximately 150 B.C. to the beginning of the Christian era—were Panaetius of Rhodes (185–110 B.C.) and Posidonius (130–46 B.C.); (3) The Later Stoa is represented by philosophers whose names are more familiar, including Seneca (A.D. 1–65), who served in Nero's government; the Roman slave Epictetus (A.D. 50–138); and the Roman Emperor Marcus

Aurelius (A.D. 121–180). The only complete Stoic writings that have survived come from the late Stoa. The thought of earlier Stoics must be reconstructed from references and quotations in other books.

The Stoics believed they lived in a material universe controlled by an impersonal, pantheistic Reason that functioned as their God. As slaves to their fate, Stoics learned the secret of the only good life open to them: Eliminate emotion from your life and accept whatever fate sends your way. As pantheists, the Stoics believed that the ultimate stuff of the universe is divine. Unlike the Judeo-Christian God, who is an eternal, almighty, all-knowing, loving, spiritual Person, the Stoic God is impersonal and hence incapable of knowledge, love, or providential acts.

One other element of the early Stoics must be noted here—their doctrine of the universal conflagration. The early Stoics taught that the world would eventually be entirely destroyed by a universal fire.[7] But then the world would begin anew and duplicate exactly the same course of events of the previous cycle. Each event would happen again in exactly the same order; each person would live again and go through precisely the same history until once again the world would be destroyed by fire.[8] According to John Baillie, it appears that the early Stoics taught "that the same Socrates would again have to marry the same shrewish Xanthippe and drink the self-same cup of hemlock; but among the later Stoics a difference of opinion manifested itself."[9]

Marcus Aurelius, a Roman emperor and Stoic philosopher of the second century, provides an interesting statement of how the doctrine influenced him. He notes how the human mind can grasp "the great cyclic renewals of creation" and therefore recognizes "that future generations will have nothing new to witness, even as our forefathers beheld nothing more than we of today, but that if a man comes to his fortieth year, and has any understanding at all, he has virtually seen—thanks to their similarity—all possible happenings, both past and to come."[10]

The cyclical view of history among the Stoics eventually influenced a number of Jewish thinkers in Alexandria, Egypt, including the most famous of the group, a man named Philo. This influence provides the connection between this chapter and the one that follows.

Does the Bible Contain a Cyclical View of History?

Some have claimed that Stoic cyclicism had an influence on the author of the Old Testament book known as Ecclesiastes.[11] The verses usually cited in this connection are Ecclesiastes 1:2–4, 9: "Vanity of vanities . . . All is vanity. What profit hath a man of all his labor which he taketh under the sun? One generation passeth away, and another generation cometh; but the earth abideth for ever. . . . There is no new thing under the sun" (KJV).

There is a major problem with this claim. Careful students of the book recognize that it is a divinely inspired account of what life would be like for humans without God. As one source explains, the book of Ecclesiastes "often seems to express a secular point of view, arguing that life is meaningless. In the face of such arguments the writer comes to the conclusion that faith in God is the only avenue to satisfaction in life."[12] What the book portrays is not a cyclical view of history but the utter hopelessness and despair of a life without God. If anything, the quoted verses constitute a reason to believe in God.

The Cyclical View of History in the Last Century

One of the more memorable statements from Ecclesiastes is the observation that there is nothing new under the sun (1:9). This has proven to be true with regard to the cyclical view of history. I will mention just two reappearances of the theory in the last century.

Friedrich Nietzsche and Eternal Recurrence

Friedrich Nietzsche (1844–1900) was a German philosopher who is best known for his frequently misunderstood references to a human "superman" and "the death of God."[13] Less well-known is Nietzsche's revival not just of the ancient cyclical view of history but also of the even more questionable belief that every event will recur in precisely the same sequence an infinite number of times. Nietzsche provides a lengthy and poetic statement of the theory in his work *The Gay Science*:

> What if a demon crept after thee into thy loneliness some day or night, and said to thee: "This life, as thou livest it at present, and has lived it, thou must live it once more, and also innumerable times; and there will be nothing new in it, but every pain and every joy and every thought and every sigh, and all the unspeakably small and great in thy life must come to thee again, and all in the same series and sequence—and similarly this spider and this moonlight among the trees, and similarly this moment, and I myself. The eternal sandglass of existence will ever be turned once more, and thou with it, thou speck of dust!"—Wouldst thou not throw thyself down and gnash thy teeth, and curse the demon that so spake? Or hast thou once experienced a tremendous moment in which you wouldst answer him: "Thou art a God, and never did I hear anything so divine!" If that thought acquired power over thee as thou art, it would transform thee, and perhaps crush thee; the question with regard to all and everything: "Dost thou want this once more, and also for innumerable times?" would lie as the heaviest burden upon thy activity. Or, how wouldst thou have to become favourably inclined to thyself and to life, so as to long for nothing more ardently than for this last eternal sanctioning and sealing?[14]

The doctrine of Eternal Recurrence gave Nietzsche a test by which he could measure the value of a person's life. When a person could approach with joy the possibility that everything would happen an infinite number of times, Nietzsche believed the person had achieved an ideal life.

Contemporary New Age Thinking and Cyclicism

As increasing numbers of adherents of such Asian religions as Buddhism and Hinduism move to the West, they bring with them the ancient belief that life is a Great Wheel from which release must be sought. For a variety of social, psychological, and religious reasons, large numbers of people in the United States and other nations have adopted as their worldview a variety of New Age thinking.[15] It is important to remember, however, that there is little about New Age religion that is *new.* Almost every facet of the movement is a revival of some feature of ancient paganism, or an element borrowed from modern alternative religions based on Asian religious models such as Theosophy, Swedenborgianism, Transcendentalism, Spiritualism, Christian Science, and New Thought. In the hands of some New Age teachers, there is just enough use of Christian language to confuse the uninitiated into thinking the so-called New Age is referring to Christian concepts rather than ancient pagan ones.

Perhaps the most obvious reappearance of ideas from Asian religions are the theories of reincarnation and *karma*, both of which contain obvious links to a cyclical approach to history. *Karma* is the belief that choices and events in people's earlier lives determine their destiny in this life. Theories of reincarnation and *karma* appear to offer explanations for many of life's negative features. The reason we are where we are *now*, such people think, is because of things that happened to us in the earlier, impersonal wheel of existence. The point is that it is a mistake to think that this chapter's examination of cyclicism deals with a long-discarded approach to history.

Criticisms of the Cyclical Pattern

The first question that ought to occur to thoughtful readers concerns how advocates of a cyclical pattern of history can come to know that the theory is true. Surely, it seems, someone would have to possess a memory of an earlier cycle as the basis for the belief that the pattern is repeating itself. Proponents of the theory believe, however, that there is such a complete lack of association between these many circles that no one could possibly possess that kind of memory.

Even if we could find a proponent of the theory who posited some connection between an earlier and later cycle, we would still have a problem. Suppose Person A does remember an occurrence from the previous cycle; that memory itself would then constitute at least one difference between the earlier and later cycles. This would result in a situation where two events that are said to be exactly alike turn out to be different because in the later case, the person has a memory of the first event. In other words, the cyclicist says event A in the first cycle is identical with event A* in the second cycle. However, they are not and cannot be identical since event A* includes a memory belief not found in A. This precludes any consistent cyclicist from positing memories of earlier cycles. So we are back where we started: How can anyone possibly know that the doctrine of cycles is true?

The only Being presumably who could know that a doctrine of eternal recurrence is true would be a personal and all-knowing God. But the type of pantheistic god favored by advocates of this position (Nietzsche, of course, was an atheist) cannot possess knowledge of anything.

A second problem with the positions described in this chapter concerns their depressing implications. It is impossible to find any basis for hope or optimism about the future. A nihilistic approach to history, such as that advanced by Nietzsche as well as by the typical naturalists of our day, declares that life has no meaning. Such a view clearly denies any goal to history. What awaits the human race is extinction and oblivion. But if human life is to have any significance, it cannot end in extinction and oblivion. Cyclical theories such as those we will encounter in Spengler and Toynbee also present a picture of darkness and doom in which the decline of nations seems inevitable. When the breakup of civilizations is seen to be necessary, inevitable, and irreversible, the unavoidable consequence is gloom and doom. The options seem limited, for there is either complete hopelessness (as with Nietzsche and the naturalists), extreme pessimism (as with Oswald Spengler), or complete resignation (as with the Stoics). In the words of philosopher Gordon Clark, "Whether we shall dissolve into atoms with nothing remaining of human hopes, fears, joys, and sorrows, or whether we fight World War I and World War II and World War III, only to fight them over again next time—in either case history can have no purpose. Neither view is entirely inspiring."[16]

In order for history to have significance, it must have a goal. Without a purpose or goal, neither history nor individual human lives can have significance. Without a goal, there would be no basis by which mere change could be identified as progress. Gordon Clark is correct when he states,

> This goal cannot be merely the end of a cycle that is to be repeated again . . . A true goal is final, ultimate, and permanent. Accordingly, if history is to be granted significance,

> something must happen once for all. The end is a unique event, and the whole historical process that leads up to the end consists in a series of unique events. There may be similarities in history. One civilization may very well pass through stages that are similar to the stages of another civilization. In this sense history may repeat itself. But Cyrus, and Alexander, and Caesar, and Napoleon lived only once. And it is only an end or goal that can give significance to these unique events.[17]

There can be no progress in history unless history is moving toward a goal. And that option is simply not available from any of the theories examined in this chapter.

For Further Reading

A. H. Armstrong, *An Introduction to Ancient Philosophy* (Westminster, Md.: The Newman Press, 1957).

Grace Cairns, *Philosophies of History* (London: Peter Owen, 1963).

F. M. Cornford, *Before and After Socrates* (London: Cambridge University Press, 1960).

G. S. Kirk, and J.E. Raven, *The Pre-Socratic Philosophers* (London: Cambridge University Press, 1960).

Mircea Eliade, *The Myth of the Eternal Return* (Princeton, N.J.: Princeton University Press, 1949).

Frank E. Manuel, *Shapes of Philosophical History* (Stanford, Calif.: Stanford University Press, 1965).

CHAPTER FOUR

THE FIRST CHRISTIAN PHILOSOPHER

The person intimated in this chapter's title was the first to make the outline of the Christian philosophy of history explicit. Many readers seeing this chapter's title might think of some early Christian thinker after the close of the first century A.D., such as Origen (A.D. 185–254) or Tertullian (A.D. 160–230). Another guess would be Justin Martyr (A.D. 100–165)[1], a pagan Platonist (before his conversion) who was put to death in Rome for his Christian faith. But the person who best fits this description will be named later in this chapter. Before doing that, it is important to examine the view of history presented in the Old Testament.

The Old Testament Background

The understanding of life and history we find in the Old Testament is an indispensable introduction to the Christian view of history. Outside the sphere of Hebrew influence, the pagan approach to history produced nothing but pessimism and despair, the natural outcome of cyclicism and eternal recurrence. Once we understand the hopeless approach to history held by the non-Hebraic cultures of the pre-Christian world, the uniqueness of the Hebrew doctrine shines like a light in the darkness.

The most significant act of God in Old Testament history was the Exodus, the deliverance of the Hebrews from Egyptian slavery. But the Exodus was not simply the end of something; it was part of a purposeful process that led first to the Israelites' conquest and occupation of Palestine and then to David's kingdom. It led still further to the fulfillment of the promises regarding the coming of Messiah.

The Old Testament prophets took history very seriously. God's power and promises were central to their understanding of the past. When they turned their attention to the future, they saw history as the drama of God's eventual triumph over evil. Their view of history occasioned their calls for Israel to repent and obey. The Old Testament prophets believed that Yahweh controls the entire process of history; God's plan infuses history with meaning. What began as a story involving only the descendants of Abraham, Isaac, and Jacob becomes, as we see in the book of Amos,[2] a plan involving people from every segment of the world.

Because the Old Testament writers believed history is under God's control, they could reflect about the purpose of history. The promises that God made in the past, combined with the prophets' trust in the veracity and power of God, led them to view the future with confidence. Not the least of these promises concerned God's pledge of salvation for those who trusted him. The notion of trust and hope towards the future shared by Old Testament writers is perhaps the defining feature of the Old Testament understanding of history.

Hellenistic Judaism and Philo of Alexandria

What we today call Hellenistic Judaism was distinct both from its predecessor—the religion of the Old Testament—and from its successor—Rabbinic Judaism. By the start of the Christian era, Alexandria, Egypt, had become the chief center of Hellenistic thought.[3] Alexandria also became home to a large community of

Jews who had been displaced from Palestine. This colony of Alexandrian Jews[4] became hellenized in both language and culture. The translation of their Hebrew Scriptures, the Old Testament, into the Greek language (the Septuagint) increased their cultural isolation from their Hebrew roots. After this, they then had even less incentive to remain fluent in the Hebrew language.

Given the intellectual interests of the Alexandrian Jews, it was only natural that they would come under the influence of the philosophies of Platonism and Stoicism that had been transplanted to Alexandria. Philo (25 B.C. to A.D. 50) provides the best example of how intellectual Jews of the Dispersion, isolated from Palestine and their native culture, allowed Hellenistic influences to shape their theology and philosophy. His writings are a mishmash of ideas, advanced largely through a strained allegorizing of the Old Testament. To get to the meat of Philo's writings, it is necessary to rise above the obscurities and contradictions scattered throughout.

Philo so exaggerated God's transcendence (otherness) that he had trouble explaining how his God could have contact with humans and the physical universe. Philo attempted to deal with this problem by claiming that God acts upon the world through intermediary beings. Philo's name for the most important of these intermediaries was *logos*, a word he borrowed from Stoic philosophers. Regrettably, it is impossible to find any clear or consistent use of the word in Philo's many writings. For example, he used *logos* to refer to Plato's world of eternal forms (ideas), to the mind of God, and to a principle subordinate to God. At other times, he applied *logos* to several mediators between God and humans, such as angels, Moses, Melchizedek, and the Jewish high priest. It used to be fashionable in certain circles to insist that the use of *logos* in the first chapter of John's Gospel as a name for Jesus reflected Philo's influence on the thinking of the early church.[5] The indefensibility of this theory has been widely known for decades.[6]

Philo and the Cyclical View of History

The philosophical influences dominating Alexandrian culture were so powerful that Philo effectively turned away from the Old Testament view of history in favor of the cyclical view. As we saw in the previous chapter, the Greek philosophers thought of history in terms of eternally recurring cycles, thinking that history is a great circle: Everything that happens has already happened numerous times before and will happen again. Such a view depreciates history. If history goes round and round, never getting anywhere, forever repeating itself, there can be no goal or purpose in history either for individual human beings or for the human race. Whatever happens to individuals will happen again; whatever humans accomplish, they must accomplish again and again—forever. The writings of Philo reveal that the Alexandrian community had accepted the cyclical view of time.[7]

The Epistle to the Hebrews and Alexandrian Judaism

The first Christian philosopher is the author of the New Testament book known as the Epistle to the Hebrews. The author of Hebrews was a Hellenized Jew, originally from Alexandria, who was thoroughly familiar with the philosophical language and ideas current in the Alexandrian Judaism of his day. At the very least, the writer of Hebrews shared with Philo a common education in Alexandrian thought. And then, at some point, he became a believer in Christ who wrote his letter to a community of other Alexandrian Jews who had become Christians.[8] The writer of Hebrews assumes his readers are familiar with Alexandrian philosophy and theology. The view that the book of Hebrews is a legacy to Christianity from the Hellenized Judaism of Alexandria is shared by a number of commentators.[9] However, by the time he came to write his epistle, he was determined to contrast his Christian convictions and those of his community of other converts from Hellenistic Judaism, with the Alexandrian philosophy that he now saw as incompatible with Christianity.[10] It would exceed the scope of this book to take the long detour necessary to go into greater detail on all this. Interested readers may find more information and supportive arguments in another book.[11]

One purpose, if not the major objective of the writer of Hebrews, was to expose the inadequacy of the Alexandrian mediators or *logoi.* The mediators of the Alexandrian community were identified with such words as Logos (Reason), Sophia (Wisdom), the angels, Moses, Melchizedek (the priest who blessed Abraham), and the Jewish high priest. Philo had applied the term *logos* to every member of this list. The writer of Hebrews believes that Jesus is superior to every mediator cited in the Alexandrian system. One of the key words of Hebrews is "better": Jesus is better than the angels, Moses, Melchizedek, and the Jewish high priest. For the author of Hebrews, Jesus is the only true mediator between God and humans. Jesus is the true Logos, the true Sophia, and the Great High Priest. He is far superior to the angels, Moses, and Melchizedek. Christ and Christian thought are better than the worldview found in Alexandrian Judaism. One way in which Christianity was superior was in its view of history, especially its opposition to the cyclical view of history that Philo had borrowed from the Stoics.

For someone like Philo, who held the cyclical view of history, events in history could never attain the significance or value assigned to historical events by the Old Testament (the Exodus, for example) or by the writer of Hebrews. By the time the author of Hebrews became a Christian and then came to write his Epistle to the Hebrews, he had abandoned the cyclical position of his Alexandrian years. He repeatedly stresses the historical uniqueness of what Jesus did to effect the redemption of humankind. Jesus "does not need to offer sacrifices day after day . . . He sacrifices for their sins *once for all* when he offered himself."[12] It is not necessary, he adds later, that Christ "offer himself again and again" like the sacrifices offered through the Jewish sacrificial system. "Instead, he notes, Christ "has appeared *once for all* at the end of the ages to do away with sin by the sacrifice of himself. . . so Christ was sacrificed *once* to take away the sins of many people."[13] Similar comments about the finality of Christ's redemptive work appear in Hebrews 10:10–14. Given all that we now know about the Alexandrian background of this writer and about the prominence of the cyclical pattern of history in Alexandria, the emphasis in the epistle about the unique, once-for-all, never-to-be repeated sacrifice of Jesus cannot be a coincidence. It is a clear sign of the author's replacement of his former cyclical view of history with a linear view, in which the death of Christ occupies center stage.

The once-for-all, fully completed, never-to-be-repeated, and final character of Jesus' sacrifice contrasts sharply with the continuing sacrifices of the Levitical priests. Unlike the Old Testament priest, whose work of sacrifice was never done, Jesus' redemptive work *is* finished. Jesus has done it once for all.

A Hellenist could not help but notice the writer's explicit disavowal of the Stoic and Philonic view of time and history. As Ronald Williamson states, "For Hebrews time matters, does not repeat itself (events happen within it 'once for all'). . . . Events in time can be decisive, crucial and climactic. . . . Events in time could never hold for Philo that eternal significance and final value they held for the writer of Hebrews."[14] The writer of Hebrews perceives time not as cyclical, but as linear. This perspective permits him to see history as progressing toward a goal, the final victory of God. The linear view of history allows the writer to see particular moments in history such as the Crucifixion as unique and non-repeatable events. Thus this emphasis in Hebrews clashes irreconcilably with the Hellenistic mind-set about time.

Five points seem clearly to have been established: (1) The author of Hebrews was thoroughly familiar with the thinking of Alexandrian Judaism and its technical vocabulary; (2) It seems highly likely that he was familiar with at least some of Philo's writings and some of the details of Philo's system; (3) The first two points strongly suggest that the author of Hebrews was an educated Hellenistic Jew, most likely from Alexandria; (4) The evidence also suggests that he was familiar with the interesting synthesis of Platonism and Stoicism taught by such Alexandrian thinkers like Philo; (5) It certainly involves no stretch of the imagination to call the author of Hebrews a philosopher, since he clearly demonstrates facility in handling the ideas of Alexandrian thinkers. Since it is reasonable to regard the author of Hebrews as a philosopher, he qualifies as the first Christian philosopher.

The Identity of the First Christian Philosopher

The material presented above provides several important clues about the identity of the author of Hebrews:

1) The author was a Jewish believer in Jesus Christ. No Gentile could possibly have written the Epistle to the Hebrews.

2) The author was a Hellenistic Jew. This means that the writer of Hebrews was a Greek-speaking Jew, one of a large number of Hellenistic Jews whose language and culture were more reflective of the Greek and Roman synthesis that evolved after the death of Alexander the Great than the Palestinian culture common to such early Christians as Peter.

3) The author was a Hellenistic Jew from Alexandria.

4) The author was highly educated.

5) The author was a great preacher. This is apparent once we realize that the Epistle to the Hebrews is actually a type of written sermon.

(6) The author also appears to have had a personal relationship with the apostle Paul and Timothy (see the last few verses of Hebrews). So here then are six distinguishing marks of the author of Hebrews. The next question should be obvious: Is there any person in the New Testament who fits this description? The answer lies in two passages.

The first of these is Acts 18:24–19:7. I will quote only Acts 18:24–26 from this first passage:

> Meanwhile a Jew named Apollos [a Greek name], a native of Alexandria, came to Ephesus. He was a learned man, with a thorough knowledge of the Scriptures. He had been instructed in the way of the Lord, and he spoke with great fervor and taught about Jesus accurately, though he knew only the baptism of John. He began to speak boldly in the synagogue. When Priscilla and Aquila heard him, they invited him to their home and explained to him the way of God more adequately.

Five of the distinguishing features of the writer of Hebrews are attributed to Apollos in these verses. He was a cultured, educated, Greek-speaking Jew with a Greek name from Alexandria who was obviously a gifted speaker and teacher. While he possessed good information about Jesus before his conversion, his comprehension of the Christian faith was deficient in several important respects, one of them being his confusion about the baptism of John the

Baptist. Apollos was discipled by Priscilla and Aquila (Acts 18:26), as well as by the apostle Paul (Acts 19:1–7).

Once his errors were corrected, Apollos became a powerful presence in the church, as we learn from our second text (1 Cor. 1:11–17), where Paul discusses dissension in the Corinthian church among those who followed the preaching of Apollos, those who followed Peter,[15] and those who followed Paul. The fact that Apollos was mentioned in the company of Paul and Peter serves as testimony to his personal and ministerial gifts.

No other person mentioned in the New Testament matches the description of the first Christian philosopher, the author of Hebrews, better than Apollos. If the given name of the author of Hebrews is mentioned anywhere in the New Testament, that name almost certainly must be Apollos.

Conclusion

The cyclical view of history minimizes the significance of history. If Hank Aaron must hit his 715th home run during each cycle of the historical process, the event loses its uniqueness. Any event that must be repeated a countless number of times loses its significance in such an understanding of history. But for Christianity, history does not repeat itself. History is not a circle; it is a line with a beginning (creation) and an end (the final judgment and eternity). Because history is a line, individual events that occur in history and individual people who live in history do have significance.

For Further Reading

F. F. Bruce, *The Epistle to the Hebrews* (Grand Rapids: Eerdmans, 1964).

Ronald Nash, *The Gospel and the Greeks* (Richardson, Tex.: Word, 1992).

Ronald Nash, *The Word of God and the Mind of Man* (Phillipsburg, N.J.: Presbyterian and Reformed, 1992).

Philo, *The Works of Philo*, trans. C. D. Yonge (Peabody, Mass.: Hendrickson, 1993).

Ronald Williamson, *Philo and the Epistle to the Hebrews* (Leiden: E. J. Brill, 1970).

C H A P T E R   F I V E

AUGUSTINE

The thoughts and writings of Augustine (A.D. 354–430) are the bridge that links ancient philosophy and early Christian theology to the thought patterns of the Middle Ages. Augustine is, without question, the most important Christian thinker between A.D. 100 and Thomas Aquinas in the thirteenth century.

Augustine was born and educated in what is today northeastern Algeria, not far from the ancient city of Carthage that had earlier been conquered by Rome and absorbed into its empire. Even though Augustine's mother Monica was a devout Christian, he himself did not become a Christian until he was in his early thirties. Augustine first had to find deliverance from several non-Christian religious and philosophical worldviews, including one called Manichaeanism.[1] His aversion to the faith of his mother was also a consequence of moral and spiritual problems. His remarkable conversion is recorded in Book Eight of his *Confessions,* one of the great classics of Christian literature.

Augustine's philosophy of history is spelled out in his monumental work, *The City of God* (written between A.D. 413 and 426).

The immediate occasion for Augustine's writing the book was the sack of Rome by Alaric and his Goths in A.D. 410. Non-Christians throughout the Roman Empire charged that Rome's catastrophe was a result of the city's turning from its pagan deities to Christianity. Augustine began *The City of God* for the express purpose of answering these charges. Before he finished, however, he found himself involved in discussions of numerous other topics, including what amounted to a Christian philosophy of history.

The first ten books of *The City of God* contain Augustine's answers to the pagan accusations. Among other things, he argues that Rome had been victim to other catastrophes before Christianity. In fact, he maintains, Rome was sacked not because it had turned to Christianity but rather because it had not become Christian enough. He presents a catalogue of the vices of Rome sufficient to make it clear that there was no justification whatsoever for regarding Rome as a Christian city.

The most interesting philosophical passages occur in the last half of the work (Books Eleven through Twenty-two) where he turns to the major theme of his study: the existence within the world of two cities or societies—The City of God and The City of Man.

> Accordingly, two cities have been formed by two loves: the earthly by the love of self, even to the contempt of God; the heavenly by the love of God, even to the contempt of self. The former [the City of Man], in a word, glories in itself, the latter [the City of God] in the Lord. For the one seeks glory from men; but the greatest glory of the other is God, the witness of conscience. The one lifts up its head in its own glory; the other says to its God, "Thou art my glory, and the lifter up of mine head" (Psalm 3:3). In the one, the princes and nations it subdues are ruled by the love of ruling; in the other, the princes and the subjects serve one another in love, the latter obeying while the former take thought for all.[2]

The first citizen of the City of Man was Cain, who murdered his brother Abel, the first citizen of the City of God. "It is recorded of Cain," Augustine writes, "that he built a city [Gen. 4:17], but Abel, being a sojourner, built none. For the city of the saints is above, although here below it begets citizens, in whom it sojourns till the time of its reign arrives, when it shall gather together all in the day of the resurrection; and then shall the promised kingdom be given to them, in which they shall reign with their Prince, the King of the ages, time without end."[3]

Ever since Cain killed Abel, the City of Man has waged war against the City of God, persecuting and killing believers.[4] It is not membership in a church that places a person within the City of God. Alluding to Jesus' parable of the wheat and the tares in Matthew chapter 13, Augustine explains that the two cities will coexist through human history, even within the bounds of professing Christendom. Only at the last judgment, which brings human history to an end, will the two cities finally be separated, in order that they may share their appointed destinies of heaven and hell. What accounts for people's placement in one or the other city is the object of their love. People belong to the City of God by virtue of their love of God; the rest of humanity belongs to the City of Man because of their "love of self, even to the contempt of God."[5]

The Six Stages of History

Augustine distinguishes six major periods of history corresponding to the six days of creation. These periods encompass respectively the times (1) from Adam to Noah and the flood, (2) from Noah to Abraham, (3) from Abraham to David, (4) from David to the Exile of the Israelites from Palestine, and (5) from the Exile to the birth of Christ. The sixth day is the age of the Church, which will last until the final judgment. History ends with the Second Coming of Christ and the ensuing Day of Judgment. The seventh day, like the Sabbath of God, will be the age of rest when the redeemed rest in the Lord for eternity. The event around which all history pivots, of course, is the coming of Christ.

Three Pagan Alternatives

Augustine's theory of history is built upon a rejection of three popular theories of his culture.

History and Blind Fate

Many in Roman society believed that history was controlled by blind fate. This is also true of many people in contemporary America. Whether it is expressed in the famous Spanish words, *Que sera, sera* or the English equivalent, Whatever will be, will be, this is an essentially pagan belief, even though it is held by many who hold membership in Christian churches.

Book Five of *The City of God* critiques theories like astrology that explain history as the result of fate and chance. Augustine opposed the pagan belief in blind fate with the Christian teaching of divine providence. As John Edward Sullivan explains Augustine's position, "everything in nature and in history, including the sack of Rome, falls within the plan of divine providence and under divine governance; nothing escapes divine foreknowledge or the divine will. Providence is a divine art which orders everything in an all-embracing harmony, from inorganic matter through living things to the events of human history."[6] The cause of Rome's greatness as an empire was neither luck nor fate. On the contrary, Augustine maintained, "human kingdoms are established by divine providence."[7]

The background of Augustine's comments about divine providence was the Old Testament picture of God, the Lord of history, who held all nations in the palm of his hand, and who of all these nations chose Israel to be his special people. God accomplishes his purposes in the creation in spite of the evil that human beings commit. At the final judgment at the end of history, humans will finally understand the resolution of God's justice and his providential plan.

History and Religious Dualism

Augustine also rejected the dualistic thesis of two equal powers competing on the stage of history. The threat of dualism was especially real to Augustine because of the years he had spent as a follower of Manichaeanism, a system that regarded evil as an eternal principle equal to the Good. For this reason, his most detailed criticisms of the belief in two gods, one good and the other evil, are found in what are called his anti-Manichaean writings.

Augustine countered that evil was not an ultimate principle but only a corruption of a more fundamental goodness. Evil could only exist as a parasitic corruption of an originally good creation. Augustine did not deny that good and evil were at war in history. But the conflict was not a struggle between co-equal and coeternal forces. Sin entered the originally good creation as a result of evil human choice and defective will. The last book of the Bible, the Revelation of John, says much about the continuing struggle between God, on the one hand, and Satan and the forces he controls, on the other. But at the end of history, God's triumph over evil and Satan will be total and complete.[8]

History and Cycles

In Book Twelve of *The City of God,* Augustine reminds his readers of how the Stoic philosophers introduced

> cycles of time, in which there should be a constant renewal and repetition of the order of nature; and they have therefore asserted that these cycles will ceaselessly recur, one passing away and another coming, though they are not agreed as to whether one permanent world shall pass through all these cycles, or whether the world shall at fixed intervals die out, and be renewed so as to exhibit a recurrence of the same phenomena—the things which have been, and those which are to be, coinciding.[9]

God forbid, Augustine says, that any true believer is foolish enough to believe that "the same periods and events of time are repeated; as if, for example, the philosopher Plato, having taught in the school at Athens which is called the Academy, so, numberless ages before, at long but certain intervals, this same Plato and the same school, and the same disciples existed, and so also are to be repeated during the countless cycles that are yet to be, far be it, I say, from us to believe this."[10] Augustine's first reason for rejecting pagan cyclicism is an argument he borrows from the author of the book of Hebrews: "For once Christ died for our sins; and, rising from the dead, He dieth no more."[11] Christians cannot accept the cyclical view of history because it contradicts the clear teaching of the New Testament documents.

Augustine also attacked the moral implications of the cyclical view. If life is to have meaning, there must at least be the possibility of hope and progress. But there can be progress only when one is going somewhere, when one is moving towards a goal. Therefore, in order for life to have any value, history must have a goal and the cyclical view of history must be false. History is linear, not cyclical.

Time began when God created the world, a conviction clearly incompatible with the belief in an endless succession of worlds, each repeating the world that preceded it. Moreover, the eternal blessedness that the Judeo-Christain Scripture promises believers conflicts with a belief in an endless series of worlds in the future. And, the redemptive ministry of Christ was a unique, once-for-all happening.

Four Presuppositions of Augustine's Philosophy of History

Augustine grounds his philosophy of history on four worldview presuppositions.

1) The Nature of God

In our discussion of worldview thinking in the second chapter, I stated that the most important element of any worldview is what it believes about God. This was also Augustine's position. Repeatedly in his writings, Augustine contrasts the God of the Christian faith with the many inferior deities of pagan Rome, along with the unknown god of Neoplatonism.[12]

2) Creation *Ex Nihilo*

Gordon Clark sums up the important points of this supposition in this doctrine.

> The different conception of God begins to affect the philosophy of history with the doctrine of creation. None of the Greek philosophies had any notion of creation . . . [Aristotle and Plotinus believed the word was eternal] . . . Christianity on the other hand teaches that God created the world out of nothing at a point in the finite past. This is an event which happened just once and forms the temporal basis of all those unique events of history to which Christianity attaches so much significance. The concept of creation therefore produces a worldview in which humanity plays the central role

> while nature is the stage setting, as opposed to Greek and all other naturalism in which man is a minor detail.[13]

3) Human Sinfulness

As Augustine says, "Sin warps human nature with the result that all men become more or less antisocial, making coercive civil government necessary; and the race, instead of forming one society, is divided into two *cities*, the city of this world and the City of God. These two societies, though they have certain temporal conditions in common, differ in their motives, their aims, and their principles; the destinies of the two cities are likewise different."[14] History itself exhibits no meaningful pattern for Augustine. The most prominent thing he discerns in human history is the presence of human sin. Later thinkers like Kant and Hegel echo his point by admitting to the overabundance of carnage, bloodshed, and greed in history.

4) Redemption by Christ

The only means by which we humans escape from the City of Man and become part of the City of God is through the redemption made available in Jesus Christ. In the words of Gordon Clark, "The special people who are citizens of the City of God derive their rights as citizens through their personal relationship to the person and work of Christ. . . . The incarnation, the crucifixion, and the resurrection of Christ are unique events, and on them the significance of history turns."[15]

The Nature and Role of the State in Augustine's Thought

An interesting corollary of Augustine's position is his theory of the state. Just as the City of God is not the Church, so the City of Man should not be identified with the State. The State is not completely evil, although in some cases, it comes pretty close. Augustine regards the State as God's instrument on earth to facilitate the temporal good of all and to punish evildoers.

Because of human sinfulness, we need a *just* civil government to keep sin in check. The State is necessary to preserve the peace; Christians along, with other citizens, are obliged to obey their rulers, except when rulers practice injustice or command acts contrary to God's will. Augustine is fully aware of the fact that many states are unjust. He draws a comparison between unjust kingdoms and robber bands or pirate ships (4, 4). He defines a government as a people united in a general agreement on those things it respects (19, 24). Both the earthly and the heavenly cities aim at peace. The City of Man provides a temporal peace consisting of mere order among humans. The City of God aims at an eternal peace of heavenly blessedness.

Augustine on Humankind's Highest Good

Near the end of *The City of God*, in Book Nineteen to be precise, Augustine offers perhaps the finest account ever written, outside of Scripture, of the final end of the citizens of the City of God.

He begins by asking: What is a human being's highest good (*summum bonum*)? What is the ultimate end of a human being? Is there any one good that stands above all other goods? Is there any one thing toward which all should strive? What is our highest good, the purpose for which we exist?

Augustine answers these questions with two terms that he regards as synonyms. First, he writes that "eternal life is the supreme good and eternal death the supreme evil. . . . We should live rightly in order to obtain the one and avoid the other."[16] Several chapters later, Augustine explains that what he calls "eternal life" can also be studied under the term "peace." The interchangeability of "eternal life" and "peace" makes it clear that Augustine has more than the quantity of life in view; "eternal life" has more to do with the quality of existence than with unending existence.

Augustine describes the peace or eternal life that he regards as humankind's highest good in the following words:

> But in that final peace to which all our righteousness has reference, and for the sake of which it is maintained, as our nature shall enjoy a sound immortality and incorruption, and shall have no more vices, and as we shall experience no resistance either from ourselves or from others, it will not be necessary that reason should rule vices which no longer exist, but God shall rule the man, and the soul shall rule the body, with a sweetness and facility suitable to the felicity of a life which is done with bondage. . . . This is why the peace of

> such blessedness or the blessedness of such peace is to be our supreme good.[17]

Of course, many who read such words may not find such a state very appealing. To some extent, their disinterest may reflect an inability to understand and appreciate all that is promised in the words. Others may find the described state distasteful because of the grip that human sin has on them.

Augustine is describing a state in which there is no pain—physical, mental, or emotional. More important than the absence of pain is the presence of positive joy, fulfillment, blessedness, in short, *peace.* Is it possible that there are those who could understand what is being said here and not really desire what Augustine describes?

Augustine not only states that eternal peace is our highest good; he also believes that God has implanted within each person a desire or longing for this kind of existence. No matter how hard we may try to ignore this longing, there are times when it still rises to our consciousness. God made us for fellowship with himself, Augustine teaches. God made us for eternal peace and life. But not every human being will achieve that blessed state. In fact, no human being *can* achieve it in this earthly life. Throughout the entire length of our earthly existence, the eternal peace that we all desire eludes us. Our mental powers fail, and our bodies grow old and feeble; eventually we die. Just as our eternal happiness cannot be found in our body or mind, Augustine continues, it also eludes us in our relations with other humans. Friendships and marriages are often destroyed, families break up, social order collapses, nations suffer from wars, there is no place on earth where we can ever be completely free from fear. People who think they can find their eternal peace in this life are chasing an impossible dream.[18]

In contrast to the lack of peace that plagues our earthly existence, Augustine describes the heavenly peace that awaits all who satisfy God's conditions:

> There we shall enjoy the gifts of nature, that is to say, all that God the Creator of all natures has bestowed upon ours,—gifts not only good, but eternal,—not only of the spirit, healed now by wisdom, but also of the body renewed by the resurrection. There the virtues shall no longer be struggling

> against any vice or evil, but shall enjoy the reward of victory, the eternal peace which no adversary shall disturb. This is the final blessedness, this the ultimate consummation, the unending end. Here, indeed, we are said to be blessed when we have such peace as can be enjoyed in a good life; but such blessedness is mere misery compared to that final felicity.[19]

One of the essentials of peace is order. "The peace of the celestial city is the perfectly ordered and harmonious enjoyment of God, and of one another in God. The peace of all things is the tranquillity of order."[20] Before there can be peace, everything must be in its right place. Augustine defines peace as the tranquillity that results from order—everything being in its right place. Eternal life is the paradigm of peace because when it is achieved, for the first time everything will finally be in its proper place.

The opposite of peace, of course, is war. It should not surprise us, then, to discover that the New Testament uses the imagery of war to describe what stands between us and the peace we all want. Because all sorts of things are out of place within us, there is war within.[21] Because so many things related to our relationship with God are out of place, we are at war with God—the only One who can give us the peace we want.[22] A number of New Testament passages describe how these wars can be ended. This theme is especially prominent in the writings of Paul who, among other things, writes that Christ "came and preached peace."[23] Paul writes in another passage that Christ *made* peace "through his blood, shed on the cross."[24] Because of Christ's sacrifice, Paul says in still another place, "we have peace with God through our Lord Jesus Christ, through whom we have gained access by faith into this grace in which we now stand."[25]

Criticisms of Augustine's Approach to History

Some critics complain that everything Augustine writes about history presupposes his worldview. The appropriate answer to this comment is, "Of course it does, and why would anyone expect anything different? And so too does every other philosophy of history." Not only does one's philosophy of history presuppose one's worldview, so too do attacks upon the Christian philosophy of history. When the battle between competing philosophies of history is joined, it must be waged on the ground of competing worldviews. We must recognize this fact and get on with the task of examining what competing worldviews have to offer, all the while testing and evaluating relevant perspectives, including our own.

Another common objection to Augustine's philosophy of history is that he derives it not from history itself but rather from the Judeo-Christian Scriptures. One major argument of this book is that *no one* derives their pattern of history from history alone, or in many cases, from history at all. There ought to be significant appreciation of the fact that Christians see something here much more clearly than many of the famous secular thinkers, some of whom we will be studying in this book. Informed Christians are fully aware of how they get their pattern of history and where it comes from. Especially informed Christians are able to defend their methodology in this regard.

While Augustine did indeed superimpose the biblical view of history upon human history, this in itself does not make his theory less plausible than any speculative system proposed by anyone else. No speculative philosopher of history (no matter how many and how loud his claims to the contrary) derives his pattern of history solely from the historical data. No matter how much data Hegel, Marx, Spengler, Toynbee, and the rest may appeal to, in the final analysis, their theories are *imposed upon* history, not *derived from* it. It should hardly be surprising that Christians who accept the possibility of divine special revelation and who believe they can provide warrant for Scripture being the carrier of that revelation find it as good a source for a theory of history as any human speculation on the matter. At least, this is how Augustine would have looked at it. If nothing else, perhaps Augustine should be given some credit for being more conscious than many who followed him that no philosophical principles of history can be abstracted from human experience. Who knows what might follow after our investigation of these secular systems is over? Once the enormous problems with those theories have been exposed, many readers may discover a new appreciation for the biblical view of history.

Augustine's Conclusion to *The City of God*

One of my favorite texts in Augustine's writings is the final paragraph of *The City of God.* It is important to remember, before reading his words, that this book took him thirteen years to complete. The work is so long that it has probably taken some people just as long to read it. But when he finally comes to the end, here are Augustine's closing words: "I think I have now, by God's help, discharged my obligation in writing this large work. Let those who think I have said too little, or those who think I have said too much, forgive me; and let those who think I have said just enough give thanks, not to me, but rather join me in giving thanks to God. Amen."[26]

For Further Reading

St. Augustine, *The City of God.* Various translations and editions are available from numerous sources including Loeb Classical Library, Viking Penguin, *Basic Writings of Saint August* (Grand Rapids: Baker Books) and others.

Roy Battenhouse, ed., *A Companion to the Study of St. Augustine* (New York: Oxford University Press, 1955).

J. Burleigh, *The City of God: A Study of St. Augustine's Philosophy* (London: Nisbet and Co., 1949).

Peter Brown, *Augustine of Hippo* (Berkeley, Calif.: University of California Press, 1967).

Dorothy Donnelly, ed., *The City of God: A Collection of Critical Essays* (New York: P. Lang, 1995).

E. Gilson, *The Christian Philosophy of Saint Augustine* (New York: Random House, 1960).

G. L. Keyes, *Christian Faith and the Interpretation of History* (Lincoln, Neb.: University of Nebraska Press, 1966).

Christopher Kirwan, *Augustine* (New York: Routledge, 1991).

J. A. Mourant, *Introduction to the Philosophy of St. Augustine* (University Park, Pa.: Penn State University Press, 1964).

Ronald H. Nash, *The Light of the Mind: St. Augustine's Theory of Knowledge* (Ann Arbor, Mich.: Books in Demand, 1969).

M. A. Versfeld, *A Guide to The City of God* (New York: Sheed and Ward, 1958).

C H A P T E R   S I X

GIAMBATTISTA VICO

During the thirteen hundred years between Augustine and Giambattista Vico (1668–1744), there were several attempts to construct theories of history. Most of the systems formulated by Christians were modeled after the work of Augustine and need not be noted here. With Giambattista Vico, a man who has been called Italy's greatest philosopher, the modern philosophy of history begins.

If one forgets that Vico antedated Herder, Kant, and Hegel, it is easy to overlook the originality and significance of his contributions to the philosophy of history. When these four thinkers are studied in chronological sequence, however, one begins to appreciate the influence Vico's views had on later philosophers.

Vico was born in 1668 in Naples, Italy, where his father owned a bookstore. He struggled with poverty and bad health all of his life, and he suffered from tuberculosis for many years until it contributed to his death. After studying philosophy and law, Vico practiced law for several years. He finally achieved the academic post he desired in 1699 when the University of Naples gave him the title of professor of rhetoric.

Vico was the first to attempt a construction of universal history on the grounds of scientific history. He thought he had discovered within history an eternal law of development. His pattern was neither cyclical, like that of the Greeks, nor strictly linear, like Augustine's. It was more of a spiral pattern that combined the recurrence of the cyclical view and the progressive character of the linear. Vico also made the first attempt to justify history as an autonomous body of knowledge independent of the natural sciences. His emphasis upon the inner life of human beings anticipated such twentieth-century idealists as Benedetto Croce and R .G. Collingwood.[1]

Vico warned historians about a number of prejudices that could diminish the quality of their work: (1) The error of exaggerating the wealth, power, and grandeur of the period of history being studied; (2) the conceit that many historians have for the past of their own nation as seen, for example, in the practice of describing the history of one's own nation as favorably as possible; (3) the prejudice of thinking that the people historians study were as learned and cultured as they; (4) the fallacy of thinking that simply because two nations share a similar idea or institution, one must have borrowed it from the other; and (5) the error of thinking that people in the past knew more about their own time than we can know today.

Vico's Principle of *Verum Factum*

Vico's work was a reaction against the view of history advanced by the French philosopher, René Descartes (1596–1650). Descartes limited the word "knowledge" to the results of deductive inferences from unchallengeable premises. The model of certain human knowledge is mathematics. Since history differs from mathematics, Descartes argued, its claims to knowledge are problematic.[2]

Vico disagreed by arguing that history works with a different method, for which Vico's Latin name was *Verum Factum*.[3] The best person to understand something is the one who made it. The historian's knowledge of the past is possible because people living in the present can acquire an intuitive understanding of the minds of those who lived in the past; they do this by examining the content of their own minds.

Vico related his principle of *verum factum* to the case of God's knowledge of all truths. Because God has made all things, he knows all things. Vico's application of this principle to history followed easily. Descartes' followers had exhausted themselves in trying to know the world which they had not made. At the same time, they ignored history which human beings had made. Since God is the Creator of the world, only he can know it with certainty; since humans are the authors of history, it follows that history is one thing that they *can* know. In Vico's words,

> [T]he world of civil society has certainly been made by men, and . . . its principles are therefore to be found within the modifications of our own human mind. Whoever reflects on this cannot but marvel that the philosophers should have bent all their energies to the study of the world of nature, which, since God made it, He alone knows; and that they should have neglected the study of the world of nations or civil world, which, since men had made it, men could come to know.[4]

The importance of Vico's point leads philosopher Alan Donagan to say:

> Vico's principle that what men have made, men can hope to know, is the foundation of modern scientific historiography. First, it defines what historians study: namely, whatever survives from past human actions. Secondly, it implicitly specifies their aim: to recover the human thinking, however different from our own it may have been, by which what survives from the past was made.[5]

One of the more important ways in which we come to know the past is through a study of that which previous generations have created, such as language, history, law, religion, and mythology. Vico clearly anticipates British thinker R. G. Collingwood's view that the historian must attempt to grasp the thinking of humans in the past.[6]

Vico's *The New Science*

The major source for Vico's philosophy of history is his *Scienza Nuova* (*The New Science*), a work that went through three editions.[7] Surprisingly, the work was not translated into English until 1948. *The New Science* has two major aims: (1) Vico wishes to discover if there is a universal law of history that governs the past (is there, in other words, a pattern to history?); and (2) he desires to see how this law is reflected in the history of particular peoples. Vico uses two methods to accomplish his aims—philosophy and philology. Philosophy is *reasoning* from axioms, definitions, and postulates while philology is an *empirical* study of the languages, history, and literature of people.

Vico's Pattern of History

Vico believed he had detected a certain rhythm in the periods of history he studied. The pattern he found is a spiral-like movement; there is both repetition and progress in history. Just as every human life exhibits development from infancy to old age, so every civilization manifests a similar pattern of development. At the point where a stage of development reaches maturity, the process of decay and decline begins. This course of development (*corso*) is then repeated (*ricorso*) in other periods, not in the same events, to be sure, but in the general framework. The general pattern is the same, but the particular events always differ.

Vico distinguished three stages in the development of any period of history: the age of gods, the age of heroes, and the age of men. The chart on the following page indicates some of the characteristics of these ages.

Corresponding to these three ages were three types of human nature (barbarous, proud, and reasonable), three different mental traits (sensation, imagination, and reason), three kinds of government, three kinds of religion, and so on.

Vico believed he had discovered the movement from an age of gods to an age of heroes to an age of humans in different periods of history. The history of Greece provides one example of this development. The Age of the Gods in Greek history is found in the centuries before Homer (ninth century B.C.). Even though the customs of the age were tinged with religion, the men of that time

Age of Gods	Age of Heroes	Age of Men
emphasis on sensation	emphasis on imagination	empahasis on reason
human nature is fierce and cruel	human nature is noble and proud	human nature is benign and reasonable
government: theocratic	government: warrior aristocracy	government: democracy
humans subordinate to deity	some humans subordinate to others	all humans equal to others

were fierce and barbarous. The people of that age believed that everything that happened was determined by the gods.

As we move to Homer's own century, we find a marked shift from an emphasis on sensation to imagination. We find the beginnings of mythical or poetic modes of consciousness, and we discover the development of language, law, and culture. During this middle period (the Age of Heroes), agriculture became the basis for economy and a type of aristocracy arose. The poetic mode of consciousness during this Age of Heroes is seen in the myths of Homer, while Sparta illustrates the importance of an agricultural economy and a warrior aristocracy.

The Age of Men in Greece coincides with the ascendancy of Athens. We now find a democratic form of government in which all free citizens are regarded as equal. Understandably, this brought about a more settled state of affairs. The culture of the time was ruled by the ideal of pure rationality. People lost some of their barbarity and became more benign.

Vico's approach to history focuses not upon individual people, not upon specific heroes and villains, but upon an entire culture. The course of the human species, Vico maintains, is a movement from a primitive mentality to a religious way of life and ultimately to an age of reflective rationality.[8] Each period of human history eventually dissolves, however, into a time of decline, decadence, and barbarism which sets the stage for a new cycle.

The Providence of God

Vico refers frequently to the role of divine providence in human history. Of course, he also admits that it is often quite difficult to detect God's providence at work in history. Human beings are selfish, and history records only too clearly the results of humankind's self-seeking. If we were left on our own, we would eventually destroy all of our kind. Divine providence works immanently within history to keep the human creation in check within the orders of the family, the society, and the state. In this way, divine providence works for the preservation of human society.

That all humans possess a corrupted nature which is manifested in the unalterable love of self is another of Vico's teachings. This self-love drives people to make their own well-being their major objective. Left to their own devices, they seek things that benefit themselves and their families at the expense of others. When they become part of a larger community, humans extend their desire for well-being to that of their cities, then to their nations, and finally to the human race. But even these appearances of concern for some larger group merely reflect the growing awareness that the well-being of the larger community is the best way to benefit the individual. Therefore, Vico writes,

> it is only by Divine Providence that [man] can be held within these orders to practice justice as a member of the society of the family, the state, and finally of mankind. Unable to attain all the utilities he wishes, he is constrained by these orders[9] to seek those which are his due; and this is called just. That which regulates all human justice is therefore divine justice, which is administered by Divine Providence to preserve human society.[10]

Vico credits divine providence for the development from barbarism to rationality. As he states, "Divine Providence initiated the process by which the fierce and violent were brought from their outlaw state to humanity and entered upon national life. It did so by awakening in them a confused idea of divinity, which they in their ignorance attributed to that to which it did not belong. Thus through the terror of this imagined divinity, they began to put themselves in some order."[11] It is divine providence, then, that makes history move.

This view of providence bears a number of interesting similarities to Hegel's notion of "the cunning of reason," which we will encounter later. According to Hegel, God uses the selfish desires of humans to work out his own purposes in history. Vico, like Hegel, insists that divine providence always operates indirectly, by secondary means. Providence always realizes its purposes in a natural, rather than a supernatural, way. Vico's lack of emphasis on the transcendence of God has led several critics to point out that his position may be unable to avoid a pantheism which he certainly did not intend to espouse.

Critique of Vico's View of Providence

Much of what Vico wrote about divine providence seems to have been written to avoid the censure of the Roman Catholic Church. But, he also seems to have been genuinely concerned to refute anti-Christian attempts to excise a biblically oriented doctrine of divine providence from sacred history. Even though he continued to believe that God had intervened in Hebrew history in specific events, Vico's handling of the New Testament revealed occasional moves in a secular direction, as when he taught that secular human customs could be a way in which divine providence operates in non-Christian nations. Christians believe that God makes history. But when Vico's mind moves beyond the bounds of sacred history, he seems to reject providence as a direct intervention of a transcendent God.

Vico seemed to be a victim of his worldview, which made it difficult for him to see how both God and humankind could be makers of history. Vico refused to deny the role of human beings as makers of history because he thought it would preclude the historian's ability to understand people who lived in the past; it would also, he thought, make historical knowledge impossible. All of this made problematic any special intervention by God in history. Since by this time Vico's worldview commitments were firmly entrenched, he lacked the ability to step back and rethink his presuppositions. Consequently, he depreciated God's control over history in order to maximize the role of humans as makers of their own history. Vico's work illustrates the collapse of important Christian convictions in his century. Despite his Christian purpose, his teaching shows how the Christian view of the past was disintegrating in his day.

Vico's view of divine providence simply fails the test of what we should expect from a committed Christian. As we have seen, he did, on occasion, write about a special divine providence that transcended the historical process and was directed at the people of God. He admitted the existence of special divine interventions on behalf of believers. But Vico's ultimate interests led him to focus on the city of man and the world of non-believers. When all his cards were played, the providence that is most important in Vico's system is immanent, not transcendent, and operates in ways that have little or nothing to do with supernatural means, even operating many times through ordinary human customs. The divine providence operating in Vico's system ends up appearing as naturalistic and secular as what one might find in a thoroughly secular view of historical development.

Pardon E. Tillinghast summarizes the more significant weaknesses of Vico's work:

> The *New Science* has glaring faults. While its main outlines stand out reasonably well, the details are often confused, as is the terminology. Vico is passionate, pugnacious and incredibly repetitive. He completely lacks classical restraint, which is understandable, considering that he feels himself surrounded by people of incredible stupidity. . . . While Vico's scope of knowledge was extraordinary, his argument is far from neat. . . . It is curious that a scientific proof of Providence should have been attempted by a man whose knowledge of both science and theology was anything but strong.[12]

One of the ironies of the Christian faith is the way, often at critical junctures in its history, people who regarded themselves as friends and defenders of the faith ended up making what appeared to be minor concessions that, over time, grew into cancers that then spread in a deadly way throughout the church. It is easy to hope that had Vico lived to see what others did with his modifications of classical belief, he would have recognized his error and changed the elements of his worldview implicated in the process. But as we know, this opportunity is never given to us.

For Further Reading

H. P. Adams, *The Life and Writings of Giambattista Vico* (London: George Allen & Unwin, 1935).

Thomas Barry, *The Historical Theory of G. B. Vico* (Washington: Catholic University of America Press, 1949).

Isaiah Berlin, *Vico and Herder: Two Studies in the History of Ideas* (London: Hogarth Press, 1976).

Robert Caponigri, *Time and Idea: The Theory of History in Giambattista Vico* (Chicago: Henry Regnery, 1953).

F. C. Copleston, *History of Philosophy*, vol. 6 (Westminster, Md.: Newman, 1960).

B. Croce, *The Philosophy of Giambattista Vico* (New York: Russell, 1964).

Robert Flint, *Vico*, reprint of 1884 edition (North Stratford, Conn.: Ayer, 1980).

Leon Pompa, *Human Nature and Historical Knowledge: Hume, Hegel and Vico* (New York: Cambridge University Press, 1990).

John Edward Sullivan, *Prophets of the West* (New York: Holt, Rinehart and Winston, 1970).

Giorgio Tagliacozzo, *Giambattista Vico: An International Symposium.* (Baltimore: Johns Hopkins University Press, 1969).

Giambattista Vico, *New Science,* trans. by T. G. Bergin and M. H. Fisch (Ithaca, N.Y.: Cornell University Press, 1968).

CHAPTER SEVEN

Immanuel Kant and the Idea of Progress

Few thinkers in the modern history of philosophy have had a greater impact on Western thought than Immanuel Kant (1724–1804).[1] Kant's most important publications, such as *The Critique of Pure Reason*, appeared in the years during and after America's fight for independence. Even though Kant's writings about history are often overlooked, he offered an important statement of one of the major approaches to history. Following a short account of his philosophy of history, the rest of the chapter will focus on the influential theory of progress to which Kant contributed.

Kant's Philosophy of History

Kant wrote several short essays on the philosophy of history.[2] All of them represent an approach, typical of the Enlightenment, that describes history as the story of humanity's progressive development from barbarism and superstition to a life of reason.

In his essay *Idea of a Universal History,* Kant summarizes his basic thesis about history: "The history of the human race, viewed as a whole, may be regarded as the realization of a hidden plan of nature to bring about a political constitution, internally, and, for this purpose, also externally perfect, as the only state in which all the capacities implanted by her in mankind can be fully developed."[3] Kant's proposition points to a rational constitutional state (actually, a league of nations) as the end of history; it also shows that for Kant the real entity of history is not individual human beings but humankind. Since what Kant calls nature does nothing in vain, he wants us to believe that no basic human desires (including the desire for rationality) will be ultimately frustrated. This means, for Kant at least, that the rational capacities of humans *will* be realized.

History itself, however, seems to teach that these desires are frustrated. At first glance it is hard to see meaning in history, for it presents a repulsive spectacle in which all seems to be chaos; all one can see are the results of human selfishness. Kant sees the same thing: "Nor can one help feeling a certain repugnance in looking at the conduct of men as it is exhibited on the great stage of the world. With glimpses of wisdom appearing in individuals here and there, it seems, on examining it externally, as if the whole web of human history were woven out of folly and childish vanity and the frenzy of destruction, so that at the end one hardly knows what idea to form of our race, albeit so proud of its prerogatives."[4] Can a philosopher find a pattern or purpose in all of this?

Kant acknowledges the obvious truth that no solitary human being manages to achieve perfect rationality. Life is simply too short. We come to the end of our lives realizing that there is so much more we should have learned. Given his commitment to an inevitable human development towards rationality, Kant can only resolve this problem by looking not at individual persons but at the species. While it is true that our human rational capacities are not fully realized in individual persons, they are being realized in the steady progress of humankind toward an orderly world order.

While Kant admits he cannot prove that history has a purpose and a plan, he says the historian must nonetheless presuppose it. Without a plan to history, we are no longer justified in believing in providence; and without trust in providence, Kant thinks, we lose the grounds for living a moral life. It is imperative, then, that the historian uncover the plan implicit in history. Given this clue, Kant believes he can discover the universal laws that determine human actions.

True to the Enlightenment, Kant presents us with a linear view of history that encourages optimism about the future. He is convinced that humans will continue to evolve towards a worldwide government that will establish peace and rational law. As Kant states, "[I]t may be hoped that when the play of the freedom of the human will is examined on the great scale of universal history a regular march will be discovered in its movements; and that, in this way, what appears to be tangled and unregulated in the case of individuals will be recognized in the history of the whole species as a continually advancing, though slow, development of its original capacities and endowments."[5]

What is the mechanism of history? Kant's answer is: "the means which nature employs to bring about the development of all the capacities implanted in men is their mutual antagonism in society . . . By this antagonism I mean the unsocial sociability of men; that is, their tendency to enter into society, conjoined, however, with an accompanying resistance which continually threatens to dissolve this society."[6] The things causing history to move, then, are human antagonisms in society. While humans need to live together, nevertheless the natural human drive towards selfish individualism[7] threatens to destroy society. The very thing that makes history appear meaningless turns out to be the instrument Nature uses to bring about the development of human potentialities.[8]

Kant's interesting phrase, "unsocial sociability," speaks both of our human tendency to enter into society and our natural inclination to isolate ourselves from others. Human beings need others, but it seems we cannot get along with them. While Kant has no use for the Christian notion of sin, it is difficult to miss his recognition of the failings of human character in his analysis of history.

Kant and the Enlightenment

Kant's philosophy of history carries the unmistakable marks of the period of intellectual history known as the Enlightenment.

Recognizing this will help the reader understand how Kant typified an approach to culture and history that predecessors had already put on the table, and how his view of history helped project certain elements of that approach into the nineteenth century. For our purposes, the most important of those ideas was the Enlightenment theory of progress.

The Enlightenment is the name given to a particular set of developments in philosophy, religion, and science that took place in eighteenth-century Europe. According to *The Oxford Dictionary of the Christian Church*, the Enlightenment combined "opposition to all supernatural religion and belief in the all-sufficiency of human reason with an ardent desire to promote the happiness of men in this life . . . Most of its representatives . . . rejected the Christian dogma and were hostile to Catholicism as well as Protestant orthodoxy, which they regarded as powers of spiritual darkness, depriving humanity of the use of its rational faculties."[9]

During the eighteenth century, the Enlightenment was characterized by skepticism in France, rationalism in Germany, and deism in England. The three controlling ideas of the Enlightenment were reason, nature, and progress.

(1) Reason

The Enlightenment was marked by an almost unbounded confidence in human reason. The natural sciences had just begun to push back the frontiers of human knowledge. People became excited at the astounding expansion of the powers of the human mind. But this growing confidence in human reason helped to produce a growing skepticism toward religious claims to truth. Those affected by the Enlightenment's rationalism became skeptical toward traditional religion, hostile toward faith, and uncertain with respect to religious authority. Human reason, the enlightened believed, could be trusted when the Bible and the church could not.

It is important at this point to distinguish two different senses of the word *reason.* (1) In its most important sense, *reason* refers to the objective and transcendent laws of logic which are indispensable to human thinking, acting, and communicating. Reasonable people would never reject this sense of *reason.*[10] (2) In the sense used by most Enlightenment thinkers, however, *reason* referred to the process of human *reasoning* or thinking, which such thinkers believed had earned the right to be elevated above the Judeo-Christian Scriptures and the historic doctrines of the Christian faith. Understood in this way, people whose unbelief made them unreceptive to the teachings of Scripture had a convenient way of dismissing historic Christian beliefs as unreasonable. In fact, all that they really meant was that the beliefs were unreasonable *to them.* In this way, what amounted to an arrogant display of self-importance was made to appear more significant than it deserved. Indeed, we could justly describe it as an instance of selfish individualism.

I trust it is clear we are dealing here with a religiously unfriendly worldview. Many proponents of the Enlightenment did not need, they thought, the help of God or of the Bible or of the church in discovering truth. The ultimate authority for the enlightened became their own intellects. Even divine revelation must be subjected to the test of human reasoning. Deism, perhaps the most distinctive religious expression of the Enlightenment, denied God's active intervention in the world. This tended to rule out even the possibility of revelation, miracles, providence, and prayer. Deism sought a compromise between rationalism and Christianity by reducing religion to a few essentials that excluded the historic Christian understanding of Jesus, of salvation, and of the Bible.

(2) Nature

The second controlling principle of the Enlightenment was Nature. The preoccupation of the enlightened with this notion, coupled with their skepticism about traditional religion, led to Naturalism, the anti-Christian worldview previously examined in chapter 2. Naturalism, as we saw, is the belief that the natural order is a completely closed system. In the worldview of the naturalist, the world is like a box with no openings. Everything that happens within the box must be caused by other events or conditions within the box. Not even God, if God should happen to exist, could break into the box and function as a cause within the natural order. Within such a view, Christian supernaturalism[11] must be false. The world is a tightly closed system that is not open to divine intervention. In contrast, historic Christian theism is supernatural, in the sense that it teaches that the natural order is not ultimate, is not self-explanatory, and is not closed to the operations of God.

(3) Progress

The Enlightenment was also characterized by an indomitable belief in progress. The enlightened believed that there was no limit to what the human race could accomplish, producing an undisguised contempt for the human past and an unbounded optimism about the human future.

The Notion of Progress

The theory of progress that developed in the thinking of eighteenth-century proponents of the Enlightenment amounted to a thorough secularization of the Christian pattern of history. Obviously, any possibility of God's intervention in the ways of the world disappeared. Nonetheless, what survived in the theory of progress clearly pointed to its source in the Christian faith. George P. Grant makes precisely this point when he says that "the very spirit of progress takes its form and depends for its origin on the Judaeo-Christian idea of history."[12] Thinkers who promoted the idea of inevitable progress retained the Christian pattern but eliminated its essential theological component. Rejecting the belief that God controls history, they touted individual humans as the primary agents. In its earliest stage, disciples of progress offered God as the ground of human development. Then, even this idea was replaced by more secular versions of progressivism. After the horrors of twentieth-century warfare, gulags, and concentration camps, however, belief in progress has been rejected by most as sheer fantasy.

The pattern of a straight line moving toward a goal encouraged optimism regarding the future. As D. W. Bebbington observes, proponents of progress believed that human history is "the account of the improvement of the human condition from barbarism to civilization. There is a striking similarity to the Christian story of man's pilgrimage between two points, but the starting-place is no longer creation and the finishing-place is no longer judgment."[13]

Even though Charles Darwin's theory of evolution belonged to the nineteenth century, it fit naturally into the mind-set that developed after the Enlightenment. Darwin provided skeptical intellectuals with a theory about the origin and development of the human race that matched such Enlightenment presuppositions as the belief in inevitable human progress. What began as an alleged scientific hypothesis about the origin of the species turned into a religious dogma that human biological ascendance would be paralleled by equally spectacular improvements in moral and religious life. Darwin expressed his belief that his evolutionary theorizing provided support for the more general idea of progress when he wrote that just "as natural selection works solely by and for the good of each being, all corporeal and mental endowments will tend to progress towards perfection."[14] Darwin's work gave the theory of progress a big boost.

The Fruit of Enlightenment Thinking Within Christendom

According to Benjamin Wirt Farley, Darwin's theories effectively eliminated "God's providential activity in nature and, above all, in the realm of human development. Man was perceived as a product of blind, random forces, that possessed neither purpose nor design. Hence, one can understand why orthodox Protestantism resisted a view of nature whose origins and future, as well as whose creatures and inhabitants, were deemed the result of godless forces."[15]

During the nineteenth century, the spirit of the Enlightenment made deep inroads into Protestant thinking, first in Europe and then eventually in the United States. It undermined confidence in the Scriptures and led to attacks on the miraculous content of the historic Christian faith, denying in the process the historic Christian view of Jesus Christ. In many segments of European Protestantism, and eventually of the liberal American Protestantism that followed, the anti-Christian worldview of the Enlightenment gave birth to an essentially anti-Christian worldview within Christendom.

While the Enlightenment did not at first destroy historic Christian orthodoxy, it did remove orthodoxy from its central place as the unifier of Western life and culture. The Enlightenment created a climate within which unbelief could invade the church and begin the process that would lead to the collapse of historic Christian orthodoxy. Doctrinal non-conformists and heretics, who formerly would have left the church or been expelled, began to teach their views within the church. To an increasing degree, unbelief began to set up residence within the church. As Harold O. J. Brown explains, "Despite the formal orthodoxy, or, better said, traditionalism, of most Protestant churches in the nineteenth century, dissenters found for the first time that they could disown basic Christian doctrines and still remain within the church, sometimes even retaining high church or academic posts."[16]

By the time the fatal year of 1914 arrived with the First World War, many religious leaders who controlled America's largest Protestant denominations, along with their colleges and seminaries, evidenced a fanatical obsession with the boundless future of the human race. The growing army of liberal professors and pastors equated this anticipated earthly utopia with God's kingdom on earth. The addition of the social gospel shortly after the close of World War I produced the additional hope of an eventual end to poverty, sickness, and war. All the while, the new religion of Protestant modernism turned its back upon the historic teachings of the apostles and reformers. Most notably, the modernists repudiated the belief that the regeneration of individual persons was the necessary condition of societal improvement.

A Critique of the Theory of Progress

The Need for a Criterion

Commitment to a theory of progress seems to support a general prediction about the future. After all, if one believes that past history provides evidence of human development for the better, then it seems easy to project that pattern into the future. The resulting optimism provides a non-Christian analogue for the Christian's hope for the future, even though the nineteenth-century hope was directed towards a secular utopia.

Such thinking about the inevitable progressive march of the human race into the future requires a criterion by which we can tell whether changes really are signs of progress. In opposition to historicism[17] and its belief that values are relative to one's culture, proponents of progress are logically required to regard the values that function as the test of progress as unchangeable and absolute. After all, if the standards that constitute the test of progress are subject to change, the defenders of the theory are left without the criterion that they so badly need. Proponents of progress sometimes identified this criterion as happiness and at other times as rationality. These or similar qualities must remain constant over time so that progress can be identified and traced through the course of history.

Moral Problems

The progress doctrine gives rise to a serious moral problem, as D. W. Bebbington explains:

> Individuals at the earlier stages are treated not as ends in themselves, but as means to the end of human improvement. Belief in progress can all too readily lead to a willingness to treat our contemporaries as dispensable in the name of some greater good to be enjoyed by future generations. Much of the bloodshed of the French Revolution received a shallow justification in the supposed demands of progress. The door is opened to sacrificing others for the sake of an imagined utopia as soon as we deny each of them the possibility of personal fulfillment. And individuals desire such fulfillment in their own right. This the theory of progress does not offer. Even when it manages to generate hope, the idea of progress confines the realization of hope to others.[18]

Since the secular doctrine of progress denies the Christian belief in resurrection and survival after death, those who live and die earlier in the process work, struggle, and suffer without benefit of the significant advantages that accrue to those who come on the scene later. Most humans will never share the benefits of the earthly utopia that is the final goal of the progress dogma. As John P. Newport observes,

> The only way out of this problem is to merge the individual into the solidarity of the race and thus deny human personality its true significance. However, as long as men live, justice will demand that those of every generation shall be able to fulfill their historic destiny and share in the meaning of history. To satisfy the cravings of the human soul, the consummation of history must lie beyond history in the new heaven and the new earth, so that those of all ages may share in its glory.[19]

Hence, there appears to be a serious question of injustice at the heart of the progress doctrine.

Whatever Happened to Inherent Human Evil?

The dogma of inevitable progress fails to address the problem of human evil. John Newport provides a helpful comment on this point:

> With all their idealisms and structures of improved social justice, human beings remain sinners in their innermost nature. However much outward history may manifest an improvement in outward structure, inner history discloses the same pattern of sinful rebellion. Pride, arrogance, and sensuality still remain. The bias to evil remains in the human heart and, as history progresses, expresses itself in the new ways that civilization provides. (A glance at the twentieth century, with its specters of the Holocaust and nuclear destruction, gives a quick lie to the idea of inevitable progress.)[20]

The belief in unlimited human progress is tied to the dogma of inherent human goodness. Once people adopt the progressivist worldview and affirm the inevitability of human progress, there is no longer room for the Christian understanding of human depravity. A human race uncorrupted by sin has no need of a savior. Under such a set of presuppositions, the major remaining cause of human problems has to be inadequate education. The world can only continue to get better, the proponents of the progressive presupposition maintained.

The liberal dream of progress leading to utopia crashed and burned as a result of what happened between 1914 and 1945. As Carl F. H. Henry wrote in 1948,

> If modern thought undermined the idea of a golden age at the commencement of human history, it came also to witness the collapse of the surety of such an age at its termination. A sky of somber shadows and unending rows of the dead obscure the vision of the future which but a generation ago seemed so bright. Had the lesson of these recent war years stood alone in the history texts, it would not have so humiliated modern man. Instead, for the identical reason that every previous world culture has crumbled, these years simply wrote *finis* to that way of life with which modern ingenuity had identified its hopes—except that the collapse came in our day with such astonishing speed and finality as to have been unforeseen by all but those with genuine ideological perspective.[21]

As the years of warfare passed and the supposedly good human beings conducting the wars continued to find new ways of killing each other, many proponents of progressivism wavered and then finally renounced their belief in progress. The presumption of progress has long since been abandoned in favor of a prevailing mood of pessimism.

The Witness of Spengler and Toynbee

Even though the theories of Oswald Spengler and Arnold Toynbee will not be reviewed until chapter 11, we can say here that their work in the years between the two great world wars pounded still more nails in the coffin of liberal optimism. Toynbee described modern humans standing atop the demolished remains of more than twenty earlier civilizations. As Carl Henry describes Toynbee's view of things, all earlier civilizations "stand stark naked in the shame of this most serious disintegration of human affairs. The two world wars have surfaced the peace-time ills of all mankind, and the picture is bleak indeed. But the plight is worsened by the realization that the long, bloody trail of human history discloses the same degenerative symptoms."[22] The record of previous civilizations points to the fact that humans lack the ability to save themselves from their fate. Those willing to learn from history must turn away from the doctrine of inevitable human progress.

Disastrous Logical Implications

One of the more important steps in evaluating a theory or worldview is to trace out its logical implications. Every freshman logic student knows that if proposition A logically implies proposition B, and B is false, then A is false.[23] The progress dogma has serious logical problems.

As we saw earlier, the doctrine of progress amounts to a repudiation of divine providence. As explained by philosopher Gordon Clark, "It was thought that if God exercised control over the affairs of men . . . or, if as is plainly taught in the Bible, he might bring the world to an end, there could be no guarantee of indefinite amelioration. Accordingly, progress must be a natural process. Whatever factors in nature it may depend upon, it cannot depend on the will of a Supreme Being."[24] If the progress doctrine is true (if A), then the development of history must proceed independently of the will of the Christian God (then B).[25] Let us call this entailment #1.

Once people view progress as a natural[26] as opposed to a divine process, they must believe that progress is eternal, that it must have been going on forever.[27] Suppose we call this entailment #2. After all, if progress began at some time following the origin of the universe or the planet or the species, something independent of the process must have started it. The point here can be seen in the case of a moving pendulum. Pendulums did not begin swinging the same year that someone discovered the law of the pendulum. And so, if humans are evolving according to some law of undeniable progress, this progress must have been occurring for as long as the human race has existed. This line of thinking precludes any possible room for a golden age in the past (entailment #3). It also necessitates that every new generation moves inexorably beyond the place reached by the previous generation (entailment #4). And there is no way around the fact that the evolution to a superior state of the species must continue into the future. Nothing can, in this way of thinking, possibly mark a cessation of this progress (entailment #5), a fact that precludes the biblical view of a divine judgment at the end of history (entailment #6). After all, if there ever were a time when the world might cease to exist, any confidence in the theory of progress would be undermined. Even worse, the stream of logical entailments means that the premises of the progress doctrine also preclude the earthly utopia so dear to their hearts (entailment #7). What the progressive dogmatists lose this time is the very attainment of perfection that inspired everyone in their movement to accept their theory.

Of course, if the progress dogma were true, then progress would have to occur in every area of human concern (entailment #8). A theory of progress that only worked part of the time and then only in some facets of human existence would be odd, to say the least. A theory of progress that could point, let us say, only to scientific development without also including human moral development would raise serious doubts about the theory.

Of course, a doctrine of progress would also require that future philosophical systems be superior to systems of the past and present (entailment #9), which necessitates that today's theory of progress will be surpassed by something better in the future (entailment #10). Once understood, that information ought to kill a lot of enthusiasm for the progress dogma. It is hard to get excited by a worldview that we know must be supplanted by something better in the future (entailment #11).

Entailments 10 and 11 point to what ought to be a special embarrassment for those who hold to the idea of progress. In one of the more important books written about the theory, British thinker J. B. Bury urges his readers to carry the premises of the progress doctrine to their inevitable conclusion. Once we recognize that a genuine progress doctrine must continue developing forever, it is difficult, he says, to find any good reason to exempt the theory of progress from the eternal development intrinsic to the historical process. Since we can never reach a terminus or an end, it follows that a day must come when the idea of progress must "fall from the commanding position in which it is now, with apparent security enthroned. . . . A day will come," Bury writes, "in the revolution of centuries, when a new idea will usurp its place as the directing idea of humanity. Another star, unnoticed now or invisible, will climb up the intellectual heaven, and human emotions will react to its influence, human plans respond to its guidance. It will be the criterion by which Progress and all other ideas will be judged. And it too will have its successor."[28]

"In other words," Bury continues, "does not Progress itself suggest that its value as a doctrine is only relative, corresponding to a certain not very advanced stage of civilization; just as Providence, in its day, was an idea of relative value, corresponding to a stage somewhat less advanced?"[29]

Gordon Clark echoes Bury's biting comments:

> If progress is the law of history, if our moral and intellectual baggage is superior to that of antiquity; and if our society and our ideas are to grow into something better and vastly different; if our imagination is to evolve to a degree not now imaginable; if all the old concepts which served their time well are to be replaced by new and better concepts, does it not follow that the theory of progress will be discarded as an 18th and 19th century notion, which no doubt served its age well, but which will then be antiquated and untrue?[30]

Even more bad news for the progress dogma exists. Since the evangelists of progress believe that human progress is fixed by a law of nature, it is hard to see how the end result and the process that moves towards that end can be anything but necessary and inevitable. Once the messenger of progress eliminates God as the controller of the process, there is no way to retain a way by which human desire and activity can have a meaningful effect on the process (entailment #12). While humans make choices, the theory of progress seems to predetermine the direction of human actions. What we learn then is that the doctrine of inevitable progress fails to explain how a world of supposedly free human beings[31] is compatible with the lawlike determinism assumed by advocates of progress.[32]

I realize that this section of the chapter may have given some readers a headache. What I have done is apply to the progress doctrine one of the major tests by which every worldview should be examined, namely, the test of logical consistency. If a theory entails conclusions that are false or absurd or unacceptable, this reflects badly upon the presuppositions that make up the theory. Clearly, there are more problems attached to the doctrine of progress than its advocates have recognized.

The Progress Doctrine and the Test of History

Is the theory of progress consistent with what human investigation reveals about the process of history?[33] One reason there has been so much interest in the idea of progress is the hope it offers for the future. But we must not allow an obsession with hope to blind us to the fact that a belief in progress is contradicted by huge amounts of evidence, especially in the past century. We have no reason to believe that humans are growing more moral or virtuous. The horrible events of this century offer powerful evidence against the belief that human nature is getting better.

Conclusion

We began this chapter by examining Immanuel Kant's philosophy of history. This quickly led us to consider the highly influential theory of progress that has dominated much of Western thinking for over a century. The serious problems of a secular theory of progress should encourage us to look elsewhere for genuine hope and confidence about the future. The Christian worldview offers something the secular doctrine of progress cannot provide, namely, a reason why history is moving ahead in a straight line. History will eventually reach its expected goal because a personal and almighty God is controlling and guiding it. The outcome of God's plan for history is assured. The promising future offered in the Christian worldview has far more to offer than any secular theory of inevitable human progress. It is not humans but God who is the ground for the Christian's confidence.

Frankly, the now-discarded theories of progress never had a solid foundation. Those who believe the Christian worldview know better than to suggest that the human species is getting progressively better in morals and character, or that humans can be trusted to lead our species to a better future. The Christian worldview's uncompromising message of human weakness and evil is realistic, whereas the now-abandoned theories of progress were not.

For Further Reading about Kant's Philosophy of History

Sidney Axinn, *A Study of Kant's Philosophy of History* (Ann Arbor, Mich.: University of Michigan Press, 1958).

William James Booth, *Interpreting the World: Kant's Philosophy of History and Politics* (Toronto: University of Toronto Press, 1986).

Michael Despland, *Kant on History and Religion* (Montreal: McGill-Queens University Press, 1973).

W. A. Galston, *Kant and the Problem of History* (Chicago: University of Chicago Press, 1975).

Immanuel Kant, *Eternal Peace and Other International Essays,* ed. and tr. by Ted Humphrey (Indianapolis: Hackett, 1983).

Immanuel Kant, "Idea for a Universal History with Cosmopolitan Intent" in *The Philosophy of Kant*, ed. Carl J. Friedrich (New York: Modern Library, 1949).

Immanuel Kant, *Kant on History,* ed. by Lewis White Beck (Indianapolis: Bobbs-Merrill, 1959).

W. H. Walsh, *An Introduction to the Philosophy of History* (London: Hutchinson, 1951).

Yovel Yirmiahu, *Kant and the Philosophy of History* (Princeton: Princeton University Press, 1980).

For Further Reading about the Idea of Progress

John Baillie, *The Belief in Progress* (Oxford: Saunders, 1950).

J. B. Bury, *The Idea of Progress* (New York: Peter Smith, 1955).

Gordon H. Clark, *A Christian View of Men and Things* (Uniconi, Tenn.: The Trinity Foundation, 1991).

Morris Ginsburg, *The Idea of Progress* (Boston: Beacon Press, 1953).

Carl F. H. Henry, *Remaking the Modern Mind*, second edition (Grand Rapids: Eerdmans, 1948).

Horace Kallen, *Patterns of Progress* (New York: Columbia University Press, 1950).

R. V. Sampson, *Progress in the Age of Reason* (Cambridge, Mass.: Harvard University Press, 1956).

F. J. Teggart, ed., *The Idea of Progress* (Berkeley: University of California Press, 1925).

CHAPTER EIGHT

HERDER AND HISTORICISM

This chapter will look at the work of another German thinker, Johann Gottfried Herder (1744–1803), and then move to a consideration of *Historicism,* the important philosophical movement to which he contributed.

Herder was born in 1744 in what was then East Prussia, what is today western Poland. He was born into a relatively poor middle-class German family. At the University of Köningsberg, he studied philosophy, literature, and theology. One professor who influenced him greatly during his student days was Immanuel Kant; in later years, however, their relationship deteriorated because of major differences in their approaches to issues in philosophy and culture.

Even though Herder was an ordained Lutheran clergyman, his liberal theological views led him down paths that would have scandalized Martin Luther; few people would confuse Herder's worldview with that of the Bible. The references to God in Herder's writings can be misleading, as when he writes: "Let no one be misled . . . by my occasionally employing the term nature, personified. Nature is no real entity; but *God in all his works.*"[1] It is wise not to approach such language naively. Herder typically followed his romanticist inclinations and taught that God does not interfere in human history, thus making history a purely natural phenomenon in a way that would have satisfied any rationalist proponent of the Enlightenment. Once again, we see how the worldview of a professing Christian is compromised by alien presuppositions.

The first part of Herder's *Ideas Toward a Philosophy of the History of Man* was published in the same year (1784) as Kant's short essay, "Idea of a Universal History." While Herder had been a student of Kant, he and Kant came to respresent different eras in the history of ideas. As we have seen, Kant's philosophy of history is typical of the Enlightenment; Herder's work is an early expression of Romanticism and is essentially a reaction to the Enlightenment's approach to history. At least five major differences between these two approaches to history are worth noting.

1. The Enlightenment began with a firm belief in the inevitability of human progress; it regarded all history as the record of human development from barbarism and superstition to enlightenment and rationalism. Herder countered by teaching that while it is possible to detect some progress in history, it is not progress toward the Enlightenment's view of a final perfect state as the goal of history. Herder insisted that the human striving we find in history is largely unconscious and non-rational. It is not, as Kant thought, a product of conscious human thought and plans. On the contrary, Herder thought, humankind in different places and at different times develops in its own way without conforming to rational expectations.

2. The Enlightenment tended to treat the past with a contempt befitting that which is believed to be barbaric and unenlightened. According to Herder, however, historians should not condemn or judge the past; they should treat it with sympathy, not with disdain. As much as possible, the historian should enter into the life of each culture and try to understand it from within. Whereas the Enlightenment tended to downplay the richness of human experience, Herder urged historians to judge each civilization by its own standards and not by the criteria of the historian. Each culture is unique and should not be compared to others. It is interesting to

speculate how Herder would have responded to the cultural relativism that is now so popular.

3. The Enlightenment assumed that human nature is uniform and unchanging. This implied that every society operates with the same ideals of reason and happiness. Romantics like Herder objected to this kind of thinking. In Herder's view, human nature differs in each age and culture. He contends that everything that can happen does happen in accordance with whatever limitations space and time may impose. A favorite analogy during the Enlightenment was that of a machine. Herder preferred a different analogy—that of a plant. Each culture grows like a plant—unevenly and spontaneously—depending on the soil where it is planted. The growth of each culture is simply a result of the right people being in the right place at the right time. Cultures have developed, each in its own way, without being determined by universal laws.

According to Herder, the principal law of history is "that everywhere on our Earth whatever could be has been, according to the situation and wants of the place, the circumstances and occasions of the times and the native or general character of the people."[2] This leads him to say,

> Admit active human powers in a determinate relation to the age and to their place on the Earth and all the vicissitudes in the history of man will ensue. Here kingdoms and states crystallize into shape: there they dissolve and assume other forms. Here from a wandering horde rises a Babylon; there from the straitened inhabitants of a coast springs up a Tyre; here, in Africa, an Egypt is formed; there, in the deserts of Arabia, a Jewish state; and all these in one part of the World, all in the neighborhood of each other. Time, place, and national character alone, in short the general cooperation of active powers in their most determinate individuality govern all the events that happen among mankind as well as all the occurrences in nature. Let us place this predominant law of the creation in a suitable light.[3]

A culture's history gives rise to its customs and beliefs. Understanding the past is always an essential step in understanding the present.

4. Because the Enlightenment presupposed the fixity of human nature, it tended to ignore the influence of environment upon human history. Herder argued, on the contrary, that whatever happens to humans is determined by conditions in their environment. The large variety of civilizations can be attributed to the fact that every possible manifestation of the human spirit will be realized. As Herder states his point, "The whole history of mankind is a pure natural history of human powers, actions, and propensities modified by time and place. . . . Why did the enlightened Greeks appear in the world? Because Greeks existed, and existed under such circumstances that they could not be otherwise than enlightened."[4]

The reason this last sentence sounds plausible, of course, is because it is also quite commonplace. If any of us had been born, raised, and educated in another country and culture, we could not help but be different. Imagine, for example, the differences in Herder's work had he been born and raised in Cleveland, Ohio, during the Great Depression.

5. The Enlightenment approached history under the control of presuppositions which it then sought to confirm in the data. Herder objected to this procedure of forcing the data of history into preconceived patterns. He insisted on an examination of the past that was free from such bias. Of course, Herder examined the past from the perspective of his own bias.

The Plan of Herder's Book

Herder planned that his book should contain five parts consisting of five books each. However, only the first four parts (twenty books) were ever published. In the first two parts (Books I–X), he discusses humankind's physical environment—the stage on which human history has been enacted. He argues that an understanding of the universe and of humankind's place within it is a necessary prerequisite to understanding history. Books XI through XX are more interesting for the student of the philosophy of history. Interwoven with discussions of the history of a number of nations are significant comments that throw light on Herder's view of speculative history. Two of the more important concepts are those of Humanity and *das Volk*.

Herder's Notion of Humanity

While Herder claims repeatedly that the goal of history is Humanity, he never offers a clear account of what this term means. Sometimes he compares history to a play, the end of which is unknown by the actors. He expects the performers in the play (meaning people like us) to trust the author of the play to bring all of the strands of the story together. The end of the play, by which he means the goal of history, supposedly includes the complete fulfillment of all of our human capacities. It is important to note here that while Kant emphasized only the development of humankind's *rational* capacities, Herder stresses the development of *all* our capacities.

Herder's Notion of *Das Volk*

Herder constantly emphasizes the primary reality of the group. History is not the record of particular humans but of the evolving social units to which they belong. Herder anticipates Hegel and Marx when he says that individual people apart from their social unit are a mere abstraction. The group is the means of individual development and the most important type of group is the nation (*das Volk*). Individual persons can receive their full justification only as a member of some *Volk.* Author Pardon E. Tillinghast offers a helpful explanation of Herder's point: "To Herder, what is real is not so much what is scientifically or philosophically demonstrable as what evolves, generation by generation, from the soul of a people, whose spirit or *Volkgeist* is the true creator of all culture in any form."[5]

Individual human persons, Herder teaches, express themselves through the groups of which they are a part. Herder broke with the tradition that insisted on understanding "liberty" as the freedom of individual persons. He regarded the group as more real than individuals. The most important group to which individuals can belong is a nation.

Given Herder's rejection of rationalism, it might be too much to expect complete consistency in his writing. He does not disappoint us in this regard. The significance of his work is to be found not in a polished and finished system but in flashes of insight that will lead later thinkers to move still further down the path he began.

Herder and Historicism

Just as Kant was a pivotal figure in the early development of the idea of progress, Herder played a similar role in the development of the movement called historicism. Historicism began in eighteenth-century Germany, largely as a reaction against various theories of progress being advanced in France and Great Britain.[6] In keeping with this, historicists rejected the Enlightenment belief that history is a straight line constantly moving forward and upward through continually better degrees of social order. There is no goal of history; there is also no place for the utopian dream of human perfection. As we have seen in Herder's case, the basic idea behind historicism is its focus on the unique culture that developed in each nation. History, in this view, emphasizes the development of different cultures. As D. W. Bebbington notes, historicists rejected the belief that "each stage in human development is transitory, without value in itself, significant merely as a steppingstone towards the further shore of the ideal society. On the contrary, each age has its own intrinsic worth." Bebbington continues by pointing out that historicists believed that every age "is responsible for its own standards. It is not answerable to posterity."[7] It is also important to understand that being irrational for Herder does not translate into passionate or irresponsible behavior. It refers to people developing in their own unique and individual ways.

Most historicists taught that human cultures are shaped and determined by history. The experiences of the larger group mold the customs and beliefs of that group. Following the lead of Herder, historicists compare customs and beliefs to flowers that grow best in different kinds of soil and environment.

Historicism's opposition to the Enlightenment's approach to history should now be obvious. A linear view of history conflicts with historicism's belief that history molds and shapes human cultures. Historicism is at odds with progressivism's belief in history's unavoidable move towards the goal of a perfect utopia.

Objections to Historicism

1. It is impossible to deny the powerful influence that history, culture, and environment have upon human groups. But historicism goes too far when it denies any constancy in human nature. This claim conflicts with the obvious fact that humans living in different places at different times still manifest similar motives, emotions, and concepts. However much individuals from different cultural and historical backgrounds may differ, they still exhibit a set of similar human traits. To claim otherwise is to oppose a central feature of the Western view of humanity; it is also to ignore centuries of data derived from observations of human behavior and beliefs.

While it is true that the Enlightenment's tendency to define human nature exclusively in terms of reason was excessive, the historicist alternative hardly follows. To contend, as historicists do, that historical, geographical, and cultural conditions are both necessary and sufficient conditions for the content of human nature is simplistic and ignores the constant features of human nature.

2. Several implications of historicist theory are troubling. Its insistence that the primary actors on the stage of history are groups such as nations has biased some historicists in favor of powerful nations over weaker ones. The extremism of some German historicists in the second half of the nineteenth century encouraged the development of German militarism. Elements of historicist theory in the early 1930s helped the Nazi takeover of Germany.[8] Historicist relativism led some intellectuals to separate the evil actions of German Nazis and Soviet communists from the judgment of transcendent moral laws.

3. Historicism's surrender to relativism now seems to have been inevitable. Most historicists failed to see how their move towards relativism undermined their own system. After all, if we lack any solid grounds to support our preferences for certain customs and moral codes, how can we justify our choice of historicism over against some competing system? It is difficult to see why the choice of historicism itself is not reducible to a purely arbitrary preference. Instead of guiding us to the truth of the past, historicism is unmasked as a self-defeating position. If there are

no objective rational grounds for choosing between customs and moral beliefs, how can there be any objective rational ground for justifying our choice between historicism and some competing worldview? Hence, we see the sheer arbitrariness of the historicist way of thinking. It is understandable why historicism's influence has faded in the last century.

Historicism and Christian Theism

No viable Christian view of history can make peace with a theory that teaches cultural or historical relativism. Consequently, the Christian worldview finds unacceptable the relativism that is so central to the thinking of many historicsts. In contrast, Christianity points to God as the transcendent source and standard of human values.

Whatever truth historicists might think they had discovered in their system would have to be relative. Hence, no historicist could legitimately find fault with anyone who found that "truth" to be false. Christianity denies that particular persons can be sacrificed for the benefit of future generations. It affirms that human beings can attain fulfillment while they exist. God has a relationship to individuals in every generation.

For Further Reading

F. M. Barnard, *Between Enlightenment and Political Romanticism* (New York: Oxford University Press, 1964).

F. M. Barnard, *Herder's Social and Political Thought* (New York: Oxford University Press, 1965).

D. W. Bebbington, *Patterns in History* (Downers Grove, Ill.: InterVarsity Press, 1979).

R. T. Clark, *Herder: His Life and Thought* (Berkeley: University of California Press, 1955).

R. R. Ergang, *Herder and the Foundations of German Nationalism* (New York: Octagon, 1966).

A. Gillies, *Herder* (New York: Oxford University Press, 1945).

Johann Gottfried Herder, *Outlines of a Philosophy of the History of Man*, tr. T. O. Churchill, second edition (London: 1804).

Republished under the title, *Reflections on the Philosophy of the History of Mankind* (Chicago: University of Chicago Press, 1968).

A. O. Lovejoy, "Herder and the Enlightenment Theory of History," in Lovejoy's *Essays in the History of Ideas* (New York, 1960).

Frank McEachran, *The Life and Philosophy of Johann Gottfried Herder* (New York: Oxford University Press, 1939).

Pardon E. Tillinghast, *Approaches to History* (Englewood Cliffs, N.J.: Prentice-Hall, 1963).

CHAPTER NINE

G. W. F. HEGEL

With George Wilhelm Friedrich Hegel (1770–1831), we come to perhaps the most important secular figure in the philosophy of history. British philosopher R. G. Collingwood notes that in Hegel's writings, "History for the first time steps out full-grown on the stage of philosophical thought."[1] In the judgment of another, philosophy and history meet in Hegel. Hegel "was the outstanding philosopher of history, as well as historian of philosophy. But more than that, he was the one philosopher who decisively changed history."[2]

Hegel's *Lectures on the Philosophy of History* were delivered late in his life and were edited and published posthumously. The published lectures are based upon heavily edited notes taken both from Hegel's own lecture notes and the class notes taken by students.

Hegel conceives the task of the philosopher of history to be the discovery of the rationality of history. Is there any meaning and purpose in the historical process as a whole? Is history more than just a series of disconnected events? Hegel believed that only one assumption was necessary in his approach to history—"that Reason is the Sovereign of the world; that the history of the world, therefore, presents us with a rational process." While he admitted that this was an assumption in the philosophy of history, he believed that he had already proven this thesis in his other writings.

Everyone who approaches Hegel for the first time needs to be warned about the unusual difficulties of his ideas and the language in which he expresses those ideas. According to one scholar, "Where some see profundity and originality in the obscurity [of Hegel's language], others see simply gibberish and nonsense. The result of Hegel's opaque writing style and neologistic vocabulary is that his works remain largely inaccessible to the nonspecialist."[3]

It is difficult to do justice to Hegel's philosophy of history without including a sketch of his broader system. But it is hard to do even that briefly and clearly. Before we approach the details of Hegel's philosophy of history, two central concepts in his system must be examined in some detail: his view of God and his theory of the dialectic.

Hegel's God

One of the more frustrating things about reading Hegel is figuring out what he means by the word *God*. One reputable commentator on Hegel provides a helpful warning: "As for Hegel's own private concept of God, it is hardly possible to formulate it."[4] But suppose we try anyway.

Hegel uses several words to refer to God, including "the Absolute" and the German word *Geist*, which is most often translated either as "Spirit" or "Mind." Regardless of his terminology, the most important problem is what Hegel means by God. Hegel at times seems to be saying that God controls history and directs history towards some divinely selected goal. But interpreters of Hegel agree about separating his understanding of God from that of the historic Christian faith. Hegel was not a proponent of historic Christian theism; he repudiated every essential tenet of the Christian view. Christians believe that God is the almighty, personal, holy, just, eternal, triune Spirit who created the world out of nothing and without whose continued providence, everything he created would cease to exist. None of this could be said of Hegel's view of God. Hegel was neither Christian nor a theist.

Burleigh Taylor Wilkins comments on Hegel's frequent efforts to associate God with such theistic concepts as design and purpose: "If the question of ultimate purpose is not a question about the purposes of individual agents or groups within the historical process, neither is it a question about the purposes of a Being or God external to the world. . . . [W]hat Hegel says in *The Philosophy of History* about discovering the plans of God and justifying these plans in a theodicy should not be interpreted as concerning the plans of a God external to the world but rather of a God immanent in the world."[5] But a totally immanent or pantheistic God is incapable of having designs or plans in any meaningful sense; such language is empty and misleading rhetoric.

Throughout history, Hegel's God struggles to reach complete fulfillment of its capacities. The Absolute does this as nature and human beings develop towards their final state. For Hegel, history manifests the fulfillment, the completion, the self-realization of God. Hegel regards everything in nature, as well as every individual person, as components of his God. As nature and humans evolve, God also develops and in the process attains a self-realization of himself in those entities and through them. It would be wrong to think of the Absolute mind as another mind distinct and above human minds. Rather, for Hegel, other minds in the universe are constituents of the Absolute mind.

Since *Geist* (The World Spirit) develops itself in human beings, it is wrong to think of history as the autobiography of individual human beings. History is instead the story of how Spirit or God develops in humans. Hegel's God is continually in a state of process, a process by which it moves beyond itself and returns. Hegel's God fulfills itself through the evolutionary development of human consciousness. According to Samuel Enoch Stumpf, "Hegel described the Absolute as a dynamic process, as an organism having parts but nevertheless unified into a complex system. The Absolute is therefore not some entity separate from the world but *is* the world when viewed in a special way."[6]

Since Hegel's *Geist* or Absolute Spirit is not a personal Being who exists independently of the world, Hegel's God hardly resembles the personal, transcendent God of Christian theism. This is a major worldview difference.

Dialectic

The dialectic is the heart and soul of Hegel's system. Once again, however, Hegel's meaning is unclear. There have been times in the history of human thought when one encounters myths that have become so deeply entrenched that the only way to explain a philosophical system is first to begin with the myth and then move towards the truth by correcting it. As Jon Stewart explains, "A handful of key concepts or slogans have come to be associated with Hegel and his philosophy in a way that lends itself to badly mistaken understandings of his view. Of course, there are times when the slogans and catchwords provide a convenient entrypoint to a notoriously complex philosophical system, even though the door they provide requires one to contradict the common interpretation."[7] One example of this problem concerns a seriously flawed account of Hegel's notion of the dialectic. One cannot these days correctly understand Hegel's position without first explaining the myth about it and then learning why it is false. Only then can we approach the correct sense of Hegel's dialectic.

The Mythical Account of Hegel's Dialectic

Hegel supposedly teaches that the world, everything that exists, is in a constant state of development.[8] The first stage of this evolving process is what Hegel (according to the myth) calls the thesis (*A* on my accompanying diagram). But a thesis is always contradicted by some opposing idea or truth or movement (*B* on the diagram); Hegel calls that the antithesis. This is supposed to tell us that the world progresses and human history evolves in terms of conflict and struggle. Then, after a period of struggle, conflict, or in the case of human thought, a contradiction, the process of the dialectic then moves to a third stage which Hegel calls the synthesis (*C* on the diagram). The German word that is translated "synthesis" is *aufheben*. *Aufheben* has three meanings, all of them used by Hegel: to cancel, to preserve, and to uplift. And so, as conflict and struggle arises in the world of human thought and history, it eventually moves to a higher stage, first by cancelling out some elements of the original thesis and antithesis, preserving some elements of the two, and then elevating the remaining elements to a higher level. But the dialectic never stops—at least not yet. The synthesis which preserved and uplifted moments of truth from the earlier conflict now becomes the thesis of a new dialectical triad, which produces its opposite, a new antithesis *(D),* which then gives rise to a still higher synthesis *(E),* and so on.

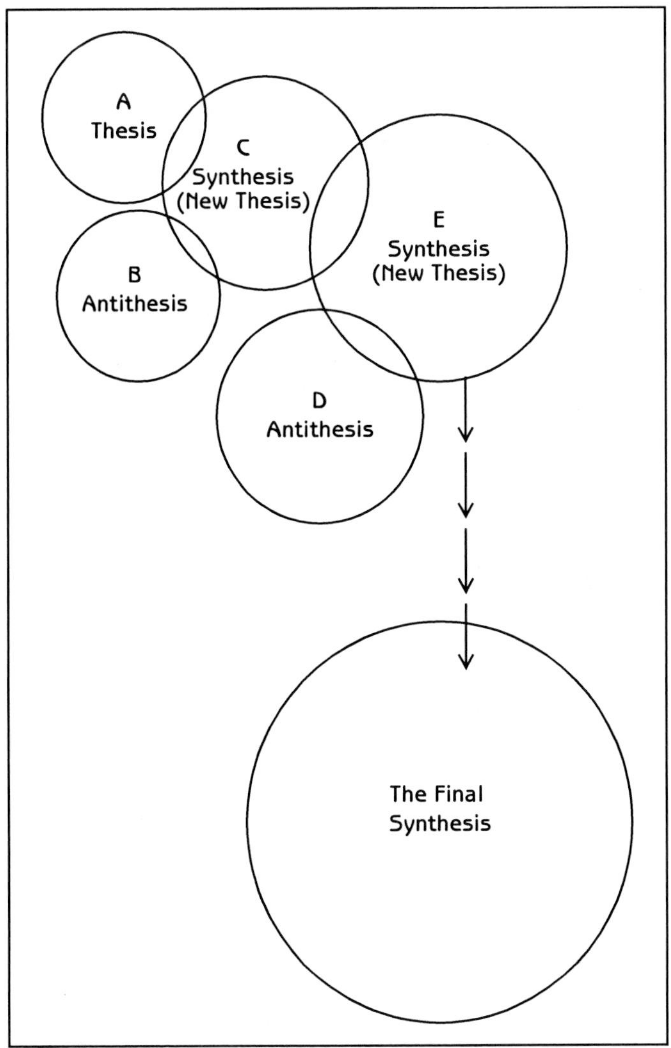

Followers of this legendary account sometimes appeal to the history of ancient philosophy in support of their view of Hegel's dialectic. Heraclitus, an early Greek philosopher who lived before

Socrates, is understood to have believed that everything changes (the thesis). He was, in the mythical view, contradicted by another thinker named Parmenides, who said nothing changes (the antithesis). To express this in different terminology, early in its history philosophy exhibits a clash between a theory of Becoming (the thesis of Heraclitus) and Being (the antithesis provided by Parmenides). But then, the story goes, along came the great Plato who offered a synthesis of Being and Becoming. Plato accomplished this by postulating the existence of two worlds, the world of particular things in which everything changes (Heraclitus's world of Becoming) and the world of eternal forms in which nothing changes (Parmenides's world of Being). In this way, Plato's philosophy functioned as the synthesis that prepared the history of philosophy for the next stage of the dialectic. But then, Plato's system became the thesis of a new dialectical triad, countered almost immediately by the philosophy of Aristotle (the new antithesis), and eventually synthesized several centuries later in the system of the Roman philosopher Plotinus.

Whenever I explain this theory to my students, I continue to draw intersecting circles until I finally reach the philosophical system that cancels, preserves, and uplifts the best of all that came before. I illustrate this last great system by a huge circle that encompasses everything else on the blackboard. At this point, I can always count on some curious student to ask for the name of the philosopher whose system marks the final synthesis of all that came before; I oblige by writing my own name inside that big circle. Fortunately, most students see the irony in my claim and we all get a big laugh. But, if the legend is accepted, we are supposed to think that Hegel honestly believed the history of ideas had reached its fulfillment in his system, which, if so, would bring about a frightening proximity between Hegel's mind and the mind of God. Obviously, it is very easy to ridicule such a system and the egotist who allegedly produced it. But is this a correct understanding of Hegel's system?

Incidentally, my lengthy example was simply the supposed development of the dialectic in the history of philosophy. But the dialectic is also progressing in art, music, theology—and in history.

Challenges to the Myth

German scholar Gustav Mueller insists that *dialectic* is not Hegel's short hand for *thesis, antithesis,* and *synthesis.*[9] Mueller explains that Hegel never used these three words together, even though he did allude to their use by other thinkers. One of these allusions to the triad appears in the preface to Hegel's *Phenomenology of Mind*, where he attacks its use by others. Mueller's translation of the passage brings out Hegel's disgust: "The trick of wisdom of that sort [the triad] is as quickly acquired as it is easy to practice. Its repetition, when once it is familiar, becomes as boring as the repetition of any bit of sleight-of-hand once we see through it."[10]

Curious to find a source for the legend, Mueller plays detective and suggests that Karl Marx picked up the thesis-antithesis-synthesis interpretation of Hegel from a minor German philosopher named Heinrich Moritz Chalyäus.[11] According to Mueller, the legend "is Marxism superimposed on Hegel."[12] Once the myth became established, history of philosophy textbooks kept copying it from earlier books and professors made it an integral part of their lectures on Hegel. It was, as Mueller states, "a convenient method of embalming Hegel and keeping the mummy on display for curious visitors of antiquities."[13]

Another specialist in Hegel's thought, Princeton University philosopher Walter Kaufmann, agrees generally with Mueller's argument. According to Kaufmann, Hegel "never once used these three terms together to designate three stages in an argument or account in any of his books."[14] When interpreters of Hegel bring a preconception of these three steps to Hegel's writings, Kaufmann contends, it impedes "any open-minded comprehension of what [Hegel] does by forcing it into a scheme which was available to him and which he deliberately spurned. The mechanical formalism [of the triad] . . . he derides expressly and at some length in the preface to the *Phenomenology.*"[15] Kaufmann acknowledges the presence of many groups of three in Hegel's outlines. But, he counters, "these many triads are not presented or deduced by Hegel as so many theses, antitheses, and syntheses. It is not by means of any dialectic of that sort that his thought moves up the ladder to absolute knowledge."[16] Few readers of Hegel come to believe in the official doctrine from their own study of Hegel's writings, Kaufmann says. Rather, he continues, "people are taught the legend before they have read any Hegel . . . and when they finally look at some of the books themselves, few indeed read these books straight through, with an open mind."[17]

Commentators who proceed under the influence of the official doctrine write as though the dialectic must always proceed, like the waltz danced by Anna and the King of Siam in the musical *The King and I*, in three-step time: one, two, three . . . one, two, three. . . . One criticism of the three-step dialectic is that it doesn't really match Hegel's writings; it's too simple, too neat, too superficial, and it doesn't really match what we find in Hegel's material. For example, the major stages of history for Hegel exhibit four steps, not three: China, Greece, Rome, and Germany.

Moreover, the official legend makes it seem as though the distinction between each thesis and antithesis is a logical contradiction. The fact is that in most of Hegel's examples, the antithesis is not the logical opposite of the thesis; there is simply *some* difference, often something minor. Kaufmann notes that the purpose of Hegel's *Logic*

> is not to flout the law of contradiction, to confound common sense, and to climb, by means of some Indian rope trick, over theses, antitheses, and syntheses, out of sight, to the absolute. What Hegel offers is a critique of our categories, an attempt to show how one-sided and abstract they are, and a work that should destroy uncritical reliance on unexamined concepts and dogmatic insistence on propositions that invite contradictions. Far from taking a delight in contradictions and paradoxes, Hegel tries to show how these are inevitable unless we carefully analyze our terms and recognize what a proposition can and cannot do.[18]

The proper way to understand Hegel's dialectic then is not in necessary steps of three, but rather as an ongoing kind of zigzag in which there is always movement and progression from one stage to another. It is important to drop any suggestion that later stages are somehow logically incompatible with earlier stages; they may only be minor variations of what went before. With each zig and each zag, the world and humanity move progressively forward to a final goal. And finally, when we reach the final synthesis (*synthesis* is a Hegelian term), all of the partial and incomplete truths that have been preserved from everything that went before reach their culmination and self-realization in the Absolute Mind.

One of the more important things to remember about Hegel's system is that truth is discovered only at the end of the dialectical process. One reaches absolute, unqualified truth only in that final synthesis, which is the mind of God. Every truth that appears in the process before the final synthesis is partial and incomplete. It may be true for this moment or be true in that context. But the complete and final truth is not attained until one reaches the final synthesis. Of course, this claim must also apply to Hegel's own system. If the dialectical process is what Hegel said it was, then we cannot say that Hegel's system is true, because the process keeps moving beyond Hegel. This is a good time to reflect on how seriously we should take a system that admits the necessity of future systems arising that will surpass the one under consideration.

Hegel's Philosophy of History

What is really going on in this struggle, in this conflict, in this zigzagging evolution of nature and humankind? Two terms summarize the answer: *self-consciousness* and *freedom*. The story of the dialectical development of the world, of human history, of the arts, of philosophy and theology, is the story of the progressive self-realization of God's self-consciousness. But what does this last sentence mean? Perhaps linking it to Hegel's idea of freedom will help.

The clue to understanding Hegel's view of history lies in the notion of freedom. Change in the world of nature produces no progress towards anything. But since history is the sphere of human change, it is another matter. Hegel thinks of history as the development of humankind's awakening consciousness.[19] History is a record of the World Spirit working out its own freedom throughout the process of history. History is a record of how the human spirit (expressed in freedom) has developed or evolved out of nature, the physical universe. Throughout history, the World Spirit is working out the form and substance of freedom.

True freedom can exist only in a rational state; it is a voluntary, self-conscious obedience to law by people who are aware of their part in their culture. These people are not forced to obey the law. Obedience is a natural outgrowth of their being loyal citizens. Genuine freedom is never selfish or individualistic; individualistic freedom always produces anarchy.

The Actors in Hegel's Drama

Who are the actors in Hegel's historical drama? They are not individual persons. History is not concerned with single men and women; it is concerned rather with nation-states. Hegel is an uncompromising holist[20] and statist.[21] The individual counts for nothing in his view of history. What is important for Hegel is that "all the worth which the human being possesses—all spiritual reality, he possesses only through the State."[22] Only in the state is humankind's essence present to them objectively; only in a rational state do they become fully conscious. Truth is the synthesis of humanity's subjective will (their own thinking) and the universal Will (which is objectified in the laws and organization of the State). "The State," Hegel writes, "is the Divine Idea as it exists on Earth."[23]

Human Passion as the Means

If the ultimate goal of history is the attainment of human freedom within the limits of a rational state, what is the means by which this goal is reached? Hegel's reply, somewhat reminiscent of Kant's "unsocial sociability" and similar concepts in Herder and Vico, is human passion. When Hegel looks at history, he sees the picture of an apparently meaningless series of events in which human beings seek their own selfish goals. Spirit uses and works through the totality of blind drives, passions, and interests of human beings. Spirit progresses as men and women are moved by their desires. Thus, human passions are the mainspring of history. These passions, however despicable they can be on occasion, and the acts which follow, should never be considered wrong since they are necessary means to an end. Even as humans think they are pursuing their own ends, they are unconscious of the fact that they are really being used by the World Spirit in the pursuit of its ends.

Hegel clearly connects God, the World Spirit, with the language of intentionality, purpose, and reasonably adopted ends and goals. Hegel's god, however, is not a person. And a god who is not a person cannot have ends or intentions and cannot act in a rational manner. It is interesting to speculate on what could have been going on in Hegel's mind. If he were fully conscious of all this, he may have thought he was struggling to explain some deep thoughts he knew the rest of us could never understand. My own best guess is that he fell victim to a problem that affects lots of intellectuals. He became so enslaved to his conceptual system at points like this that he lost the ability to step back and think critically about what he was writing. That is one of the ways worldviews work.

The Cunning of Reason

Hegel, echoing Kant, admits that history presents us with discouraging scenes of murder, mayhem, vice, and greed which seem to contradict his claim that history is a meaningful, goal-directed process. Even though history is "the slaughter bench at which the happiness of peoples, the wisdom of states, and the virtues of individuals have been victimized,"[24] all this carnage is part of the World Spirit's process of self-realization. All the distress, defeat, suffering, and sacrifice of history are the very means by which freedom develops. In the depressing record of tragedy, heartbreak, and stupidity is to be found the mechanism of history. Hegel calls this "the cunning of reason."[25] Individual men and women—their dreams, hopes, ambitions, and happiness—are grist to Freedom's mill. Only the Universal or the State (as opposed to individual persons) is real. The individual and the particular must perish; the rights and liberties of individual people are destroyed. But through the destruction of such individual persons, the Universal is realized.

Hegel's Heroes

Whenever the World Spirit must initiate new and difficult turns in human history, it makes use of certain individuals whom Hegel calls "heroes." These world-historical persons are those who seem to grasp a higher universal, make it their own purpose, and realize it in accordance with the Spirit's higher law. They think that they are merely following their own desires. They have no consciousness of the Spirit itself. But in reality, their own particular purposes contain substantially the will of the World Spirit.

While these heroes are not aware of the Spirit as such, while they think they are only working for their own satisfaction, they nonetheless have their finger on the pulse of the time. They know what things are needed; they are the leaders of their age. But they can never be happy, for they are always in breathless pursuit of what they take to be their own aim in life. In Hegel's words, "Their whole life was labor and trouble, their whole nature was naught else but their Master Passion. When their object is attained, they fall off like empty hulls from the kernel."[26] Alexander the Great died young, Julius Caesar was murdered, and Napoleon was exiled to Saint Helena. The world-historical individual is not considerate. He[27] drives relentlessly toward his one purpose, often crushing down, as he would helpless flowers, many innocent individuals in his path.

The Stages in History

Things in the world of nature are attracted to other things, to things that exist independently of them. An apple falling from a tree is attracted towards the center of the earth. But when we turn to the realm of *Geist* or spirit or mind, we encounter something that is self-contained. Because humans can participate in Spirit, they possess autonomy in the sense that they act freely, they choose what they will do, and those choices involve things that often do not exist in the world of nature. When humans act freely, in the sense of freedom that is most important for Hegel, they advance self-consciousness in their nation.

Hegel draws an important distinction between two senses of freedom. For many people, what they think of as freedom is really just capricious behavior. Such people think they are free when they simply do whatever they want. For Hegel, however, only certain kinds of behavior advance freedom. Freedom under law can differ greatly among different people. Different eras of history manifest different degrees of freedom which become incarnate in one nation at a time. The development of freedom in human history can be seen in different stages.

Hegel first draws attention to the nations of the East, such as China and India. He speaks of them as "the immersion of Spirit in natural life." The State appeared first in them as an immediate, natural unity—as a despotism. Because the form of government was an absolute monarchy, freedom in such Asian states was merely potential. Because they did not know that universal man[28] was free, they were not free. Even the ruler, the despot, was not free since true freedom can exist only under law. The freedom of the despot was merely caprice.

As time passed, individuals became more conscious of their potentialities and began to organize their relationships in accordance with reason. The scene shifted from the Orient to the Mediterranean; the principal units of history became the nations of Greece and Rome. In place of a despotism, the form of government was now democratic or aristocratic. No longer was just one man free; there was now some measure of individual freedom. The important innovation among the Greeks was the introduction of the notion of law. Social order thus was transformed into the dialectical tension between law and citizen, between universal (in this case, law) and particular (individual people). But the Greeks only knew that some men were free, not that man, the universal, was free.[29] Since only some were subject to law in Greece, the essential rights of all people were not yet recognized. Therefore, freedom for the Greeks was an accident.

In Hegel's own Christian Germany, he believed, the state rose out of the particular forms of freedom existing in the past into universal freedom. In the constitutional governments of his day, all men were free. There was "one lord and no serf" because humans willingly submerged themselves in the universal idea.

Two Problems

Given Hegel's belief that history is a rational process moving inevitably towards a particular goal, does it not follow for him that everything that happens is justified by the mere fact that it happens? Despite all of Hegel's talk about blood and gore in history, it does seem as if he dismisses all too casually the problem of evil in history. Hegel's system serves as a rationale for whatever evil happens to exist. This is an unmitigated justification of the status quo. Whatever is, is good. Whatever is, is justified.

Another serious problem in Hegel's view of history is his disdain for individual persons. Many philosophers of history have argued that history is properly concerned with something other than individual human beings. In several of the systems studied in this book, the individual counts for little or nothing. In Marx's theory, all history is the history of classes and their continuing struggle with each other. Herder regarded the individual apart from his social unit as a mere abstraction. And this also was true of Hegel's system: Individual humans are but pawns in the inevitable movement of history toward the Universal.

Were these philosophers correct when they discounted the importance of the individual and sought to explain history in terms of the social groups to which humans belonged? Is Herder's *das Volk*, or Kant's nation, or Hegel's state, or Marx's class, or Spengler's culture the basic unit of history? Or is it individual human beings and their relationship with God?

For Further Reading

W. H. Dray, *Philosophy of History* (Englewood Cliffs, N.J.: Prentice-Hall, 1964).

J. N. Findlay, *Hegel: A Re-Examination* (Brookfield, Vt.: Ashgate, 1993).

G. W. F. Hegel, *The Philosophy of History*, tr. J. Sibree [1858] (New York: Dover, 1953).

G. W. F. Hegel, *The Philosophy of Hegel*, ed. Carl H. Friedrich, (New York: Modern Library, 1954).

G. W. F. Hegel, *Reason in History,* ed. R. S. Hartman (New York: Liberal Arts Press, 1953), an edited translation of the *Introduction to Hegel's Lectures on the Philosophy of History.*

Sidney Hook. *From Hegel to Marx* (Ann Arbor, Mich.: University of Michigan Press, 1962).

Walter Kaufmann, *Hegel, A Reinterpretation* (New York: Doubleday, 1966).

Frank Manuel, *Shapes of Philosophical History* (Stanford, Calif.: Stanford University Press,1965).

G. R. G. Mure, *An Introduction to Hegel* (Westport, Conn.: Greenwood Press, 1982).

W. T. Stace, *The Philosophy of Hegel* (New York: Dover, 1955).

Burleigh Taylor Wilkins, *Hegel's Philosophy of History* (Ithaca, N.Y.: Cornell University Press, 1974).

CHAPTER TEN

KARL MARX

This chapter explains and evaluates what we might call the classic Marx, the understanding of Marx's thought that dominated discussions of his beliefs outside the orbit of influence controlled by Lenin, Stalin, and Mao Tse Tung since the 1848 publication of *The Communist Manifesto*. Anyone who seriously tried to maintain that the views of Lenin, Stalin, Mao, or even Castro, were a faithful representation of Marx's thought would be immediately disqualified as a serious student of Marx.

In the last few decades of the twentieth century, new forms of Marxian thought have arisen that sometimes pretend Marx himself never taught the theories discussed in this chapter. Some members of these groups will claim that too much of what is said here is spent attributing a long-outdated set of beliefs to Marx. This claim is disingenuous. Marx *did* teach the views attributed to him in this chapter. It is important that future generations understand fully what the founder of Marxism really taught, no matter how embarassing those claims might be for later Marxists. The kind of historical revisionism practiced by many modern Western Marxists attempts to rewrite history to eliminate the classic Marx from the history of ideas. This chapter reports what Marx did in fact teach, while occasionally tossing into the salad elements of the early revisionist attempts of Lenin and others. In chapter 12, I will revisit the Marxian arena to look at several recent attempts to reinterpret Marx for post-World War II readers.

Marx's Worldview

Marx's worldview is vintage naturalism. The account of naturalism found in chapter 2 of this book fits Marx perfectly; all of the objections to naturalism in that chapter also apply to Marx.

As we saw in chapter 2, worldviews can be identified in terms of six collections of beliefs. The first, the question of God's existence and nature, can be handled quickly in Marx's case: He was an atheist. Regarding ultimate reality, Marx was a materialist. On the third worldview issue, the theory of knowledge, Marx had little or no idea how his atheistic materialism made logical demands on his other worldview beliefs. His theory of knowledge is that he really had no theory of knowledge. Marx seemed not to recognize that his naturalism made any knowledge claim problematic. He continued his work, making all kinds of knowledge claims, without realizing how his discovery of the "truth" about anything really was a kind of miracle.

In his book *Intellectuals,* historian Paul Johnson documents Marx's propensity to distort the truth in his writings. Marx did not simply misquote his sources, Johnson contends; it is obvious that he did so knowingly and intentionally in an effort to give his untenable claims an appearance of plausibility. "The truth is," Johnson writes, "even the most superficial inquiry into Marx's use of evidence forces one to treat with scepticism everything he wrote which relies on factual data. He can never be trusted. The whole of the key chapter 8 of *Capital* is a deliberate and systematic falsification to prove a thesis which an objective examination of the facts showed was untenable."[1]

Just as in folklore, all cretins are liars, so in ethics, all naturalists are relativists;[2] and Marx does not surprise us. Like most naturalists, Marx repeatedly makes moral judgments that have a ring of absoluteness and authoritarianism about them. When Marx condemns the rich and powerful who oppress others, for example, he really sounds like someone describing an objective moral evil that everyone should see. As for Marx's theory of human nature, a consistent naturalist would have viewed humans as just another, somewhat advanced variety of animal life. But Marx professes a special moral concern about those who do not own private property or the means of production.

The Classic Marx

Karl Marx (1818–83) began his intellectual career as a disciple of Hegel. As Sidney Hook explains, "No two names are at once so suggestive of both agreement and opposition as are the names Hegel and Marx. . . . No one can plausibly call into question the historical influence of Hegel upon the formation of Marx's thought. That has been amply documented by Marx himself in published and unpublished writings."[3] As Marx's views developed, his writings also revealed an increasing indebtedness to the thought of Ludwig Feurbach, the German materialist, and to others like Saint Simon, who influenced Marx's social and economic views.

For many years, a theory called Economic Determinism was attributed to Marx. The label refers to Marx's early conviction that all aspects of human life (political, aesthetic, religious, scientific, and historical) are determined by the ways in which humans make a living. The most important factor in explaining human history is an economic one.

Textual support for a raw, unsophisticated type of economic determinism seems clearly present in the preface to Marx's *A Contribution to the Critique of Political Economy,* where he writes: "The mode of production in material life determines the general character of the social, political, and spiritual processes of life. It is not the consciousness of men that determines their existence, but, on the contrary, their social existence determines their consciousness."[4]

Understood literally, Marx's words report that economics is the *only* factor determining human life. As philosopher Sidney Hook summarizes the issue, Marx "asserted that, broadly speaking, the economic structure of society and its changes were the independent variables out of which all other cultural changes were a function. Or more simply put, the economic structure of society determines the life of any society in historic times."[5]

Such a theory would require us to believe that the music of Mozart, the art of Michelangelo, and the religion of Moses were causally determined, made necessary by the economic conditions of their time, an obviously absurd claim. D. W. Bebbington offers his own negative evaluation of this doctrine. It is difficult to believe, he writes, "that great works of art simply reflect—however remotely—the way men labour for food, clothing and shelter. Marxism offers little explanation of the timeless appeal of Shakespeare to people in societies with entirely different modes of production. Nor, more importantly for our purposes, does it explain why artistic achievements took place when they did . . . It is difficult . . . to see how the economic development of society can be seen as the ultimately determining factor behind artistic achievement."[6]

Economic determinism, the claim that the *only* factor determining human thought and life is economic, is so easy to refute that following Marx's death, his collaborator, Friedrich Engels, attempted to change the subject. Claiming that Marx would never have been so foolish as to teach economic determinism, Engels insisted that Marx only meant to teach that economic conditions are the *most important* of many influences upon human and cultural life. This revised position came to be known as Historical Materialism.[7] Even though Engels' revisionism on this point eventually won the day among the faithful, the textual evidence supporting economic determinism in Marx's thinking is hard to ignore.

Marx and the Dialectic

As noted in the last chapter, Marx appears to have been a major player in propagating the myth of Hegel's three-stage dialectic. To review this, one event or truth (a thesis) is negated by a contrary event or truth (antithesis). Out of this conflict arises a higher truth (synthesis), which preserves something of each prior truth and raises it to a higher level. As we have seen, Hegel was a philosopher of process and change who emphasized conflict and struggle.

But a serious problem arises in connection with Marx's insistence that the development always and necessarily occurs through the alleged three-step dialectic. Once the myth[8] gained a following in Marx's circles, it was a simple matter to turn Hegel's supposed dialectic into a three-stage process of change and development affecting all of reality. This change took place by means of strife, conflict, and contradiction.

Hegel's system was a form of philosophical idealism and a plea for political accommodation. Pretending to turn Hegelianism rightside up, Marx replaced Hegel's idealism with his own materialism, thus creating his now famous "dialectical materialism." Marx also replaced Hegel's political quietism and accommodationism with his own activism and call for social revolution. When Marx was finished, *his* dialectic became his tool for studying history. He wanted to explain the conflict and opposition he found in history, and the dialectic gave him the clue he needed.

Marx claimed that history was his teacher. However, it is clear that he came to his study of history already presupposing the principle of the dialectic he believed he had learned from Hegel. Reading history through the filter of his presuppositions, he came away from history with his theory of the class struggle and the state.

Marx and the Class Struggle

Like Hegel and Kant before him, Marx wrote that at first glance there appears to be no meaning to history. As we view the conflicts between members of society, the contradictions of social life, and the struggles between individuals, societies, and nations, all seems to be chaos. As Lenin commented when he read Marx early in the twentieth century, "Marxism provides a clue which enables us to discover the reign of law in this seeming labyrinth and chaos: the theory of the class struggle . . . The conflict of strivings arises from differences in the situation and modes of life of the classes into which society is divided."[9]

As Marx and Engels point out in their joint work, *The Communist Manifesto,* "the whole history of mankind has been a history of class struggles, contests between exploiting and exploited, ruling and oppressed classes . . . The history of all hitherto existing society is the history of class struggle." History, they reported, tells the story of the continuing struggle between "The Haves" and "The Have-Nots."[10] The exploitation of the Have-Nots by the Haves has taken different forms at different times, but it has always been the result of the economic situation of the time.

In ancient history, the class struggle took the form of slavery. The Haves were the slaveowners, the Have-Nots were the slaves. The exploitation centered around private property—in this case, the slave himself. During the middle ages, the struggle assumed the form of feudalism. At stake was ownership of the land: the Haves were the landowners and the Have-Nots were the serfs. Finally, in Marx's own day, the class struggle had assumed the form of capitalism. Now the bourgeoisie (the owners of the means of production) confronted the proletariat (the wage earners) in what Marx was convinced would be a fight to the death. The bourgeois exploitation of the proletariat under capitalism had produced many social evils which Marx and others criticized. Marx went beyond most of the social critics of his time, however, and argued that ending the evils of the class struggle mandated a change in who controlled the instruments of production. Private property must be abolished, and other changes just as drastic must be introduced.

Revolution

If private property is the basis of oppression and conflict in human history, then ending that oppression requires the elimination of its cause. This cannot be done easily. No significant change in this regard can be brought about without the overthrow of the state, and this means revolution. Marx held that the state is evil because the bourgeoisie uses it to exploit and oppress the proletariat. When the class struggle finally ends in the triumphant proletarian overthrow of the bourgeoisie, society will become classless and the need for the state will vanish, causing it to wither away. Accordingly, Marx declares that the first task of the proletarian revolution is the capture and destruction of the bourgeois state.

Marx's doctrine of the revolution is one of the more ambiguous aspects of his system. His followers disagreed over whether the revolution must be violent. Some, like the British Fabians and the German Social Democrats, argued that the revolution could be brought about by peaceful means.[11] This disagreement even existed in Russia, where Lenin's Bolsheviks accused the more moderate Mensheviks of distorting and omitting the revolutionary side of Marx's teachings.

Marx blundered when he came to predict the time of the revolution. As late as 1859, he believed that "no social order ever disappears before all the productive forces, for which there is room in it, have been developed; and new higher relations of production never appear before the material conditions of their existence have matured in the womb of the old society."[12] Marx surely meant here that a proletarian revolution cannot occur without a proletariat. But before there can be a proletariat, capitalism must exist. Yet in many nations of Marx's day, including Russia, feudalism still existed. Therefore, Marx argued that in those countries where industrialization was proceeding unevenly or slowly, the proletariat would have to assist the development of capitalism before they could dare begin their own revolution. A bourgeois revolution destroying any remnants of feudalism would have to occur before the proletarian revolution. According to E. H. Carr, the belief that the proletarian revolution had to await the complete development of capitalism "was the view seriously propounded by Russian Marxists, Bolsheviks and Mensheviks alike, down to 1905—perhaps even down to 1917. Meanwhile, however, in the Spring of 1905, Lenin's practical mind worked out a new scheme under which the proletariat was to seize power in conjunction with the peasantry, creating a 'democratic dictatorship' of workers and peasants; and this became the official doctrine of the October Revolution."[13]

Near the end of his life, Marx did admit that the full development of capitalism might not be necessary in predominantly peasant countries like Russia. While this was an interesting concession to expediency, it was hardly consistent with the historical pattern he had claimed to find earlier in his life.

The purpose of the proletarian revolution was to begin the equalization of wealth and put an end to the injustices found in capitalism. But even a successful proletarian revolution would not automatically usher in the classless society. Marx believed that capitalism was too well entrenched. After the revolution, at least two more steps would have to be taken toward the goal of a communist society: the dictatorship of the proletariat and the withering away of the state.

The Dictatorship of the Proletariat

After the proletarian revolution, the state would be controlled by the proletariat and would be used as a means of coercion and oppression in destroying any remnants of capitalism. Marx's name for this temporary proletarian state was "the dictatorship of the proletariat." Marx regarded the dictatorship of the proletariat as a transition period between capitalism and the classless society. Neither he nor Engels, however, had much to say about its nature or about the exact conditions under which this proleterian state finally would be abolished. Engels did write that when the time was ripe, the state would "wither away."

After Lenin gained control of the Russian revolution in October 1917, he made a number of tactical errors that brought the Russian economy to the brink of ruin.[14] He admitted that Russia was not yet ready for the classless society, a feat made easy by the fact that Bolshevik Russia was rapidly falling apart. And so Lenin emphasized Marx's phrase, "the dictatorship of the proletariat," and used it to justify the drastic controls he imposed upon the parts of Russia controlled by the Red Army. While Marx had thought of the dictatorship of the proletariat as a kind of worker's democracy, Lenin turned it into a dictatorship of the small, exclusivist communist party over the proletariat. Of course, as time passed, even the Russian Communist party came under the control of the smaller central committee, and eventually under the domination of the tyrant dictator Josef Stalin. Every level of Soviet society, including the peasants, the workers, members of the Communist party, and even the central committee, was controlled by Stalin.

It is important to see how Marx's picture of history combined elements of both the cyclical and linear views of history. The cyclical element appears in the repetition of the life-and-death struggle between the Haves and the Have-Nots. The linear aspect is seen in the inevitable movement of history towards the final revelation which supposedly would prepare the world for the classless society. Curious readers should investigate whether Marx or

Lenin ever gave a reason why this movement suddenly and necessarily must end when it finally reaches the stage when Marxists are in control.

Some Objections

Sidney Hook was one of America's better known philosophers after World War II. His criticisms of Marx reflect the thinking of many scholars of that period. Hook's disregard for Marx's scholarship is evident when he writes, "Rigorous examination is one thing Marx's ideas will not stand because they were not rigorously formulated . . . They contain a mixture of the true, the vague, and the false."[15] Hook points out, for example, that Marx's writings fail to explain the change from feudalism to capitalism.[16]

Hook shows little respect for the theory of historical materialism. He believed that Marx's attempt to explain the major cultural and political developments in a society as effects of economic factors is a dismal failure. Historical materialism also neglects to explain why similar economic institutions in different nations are compatible with significantly different forms of political organization. Historical materialism, Hook contends, "is not intelligible and serves only as an excuse to avoid thought about troublesome questions."[17]

Additional problems arise in connection with Marx's claim that no social order ever disappears before all of the potential productive forces within it have developed. According to Hook, it is difficult "to see why any social system not destroyed by war or natural disaster, should perish . . . Slavery would not have disappeared until it had at least become universal. Capitalism might keep on going by opening new frontiers of need requiring new industries for their gratification. Theoretically, human ingenuity under any system can build contrivance upon contrivance to develop productive forces."[18] Nor did Marx, Hook argues, ever make a convincing case for his assertion that "capitalism *must* be followed by socialism rather than *other* forms of society."[19]

Focusing on Marx's beliefs that the communist state would someday disappear ("wither away") and that the distribution of goods under socialism will be based exclusively upon need,[20] Hook dismisses the theories as sheer Utopianism.[21] "In a world,"

Hook writes, "where it is technically impossible to produce more than enough of everything *at the same time*, the proposal to distribute goods and services in accordance with need alone is unworkable. Needs are indefinite, subjective, and potentially unlimited."[22]

Marx also ignored the frequency with which beliefs and moral causes can motivate people to act in ways that are contrary to normal economic incentives. Slavery did not officially end in England in 1807 because slave plantations in the West Indies began losing money, but because religious and moral attacks upon the practice affected the public conscience. Clearly Marx's emphasis upon economic considerations as the primary cause of social and cultural conditions was simplistic.

There is no need here to critique Marxian economics and its dismal record of economic failure; I have done that elsewhere.[23] Those failures are not just occasional or incidental consequences of Marxian economics; they are a necessary byproduct of a system that eliminates uncoerced market exchanges and the steady stream of essential information that genuine markets supply to astute observers. Socialism is an economic theory that makes rational economic behavior impossible.

Marx's view of the future failed to develop according to his plan. The worldwide revolution Marx predicted never occurred; indeed, no proletarian revolution ever occurred from within as Marx predicted it would. Marx also failed to see the flexibility that would allow capitalism to adapt to changing conditions. Nor could anyone pretend that all the evils perpetrated by the rulers, the secret police, the corrupt court systems, and the military in Marxist states never existed. Was it an accident that wherever Marxism reigned the alleged pursuit of a totally free society ended up enslaving people?

Classical Marxism stumbled over the same moral problem as the progress dogma. The best Marxism could offer in the way of human fulfilment was sacrifice and effort for the benefit of those not yet born. Under rulers like Stalin, Marx's theory turned into a reality where coercive regimes violated the rights and forfeited the lives of millions of people; these sacrifices were a means to the ends of a few powerful people. One could hardly have opposed

Stalinist tyranny with an appeal to Marx's naturalism and moral relativism.

Marx's theories cannot be viewed as merely incidental to the evils of Bolshevism, especially the deplorable record on human rights so visible in Marxist states. In a 1998 article, eminent French historian Alain Besancon notes how leftist intellectuals lose control when anyone suggests "that Bolshevism and Nazism are related phenomena; fraternal twins . . ."[24] As Besancon continues:

> These two monstrous ideologies, each a bastard offshoot of German Romantic philosophy, came to power in the 20th century, and each took it as its goal to bring about a perfect society by uprooting the element of evil that stood in its way. In the case of Communism, the malignancy was defined as property . . . In the case of Nazism, the malignant principle was located in the so-called inferior races, first and foremost the Jews.[25]

In their attempt to deal with the evil they claimed to see in their societies, Besancon notes that "both Communism and Nazism drew their authority from science. They were creating a 'new man,' and to this end they proposed to reeducate all of humanity." This they did, he explains, "in the name of those selfsame ideals that Nazism and Communism alike arrogated to themselves, the right to murder whole categories of men, which is exactly what they proceeded to do upon assuming power, and on a scale previously unknown in history. And that is why it is proper to judge them both, in their very nature, as criminal systems."[26]

It is impossible to escape the difficulty that naturalists, including Marx, have with moral theory. As the Russian novelist Fyodor Dostoyevsky made clear, "If there is no God, everything is permitted." When a group of people adopt a worldview that has no place for a personal and moral God, we should not be surprised to find that the notions of good and evil lose their power. While atheists may acknowledge moral principles, they cannot provide good *reasons* for them. And when this situation exists, their commitment to those standards is bound to be more loose than for people who have a rational ground for their standards. As theologian John Frame observes:

> To say God exists is to say that the world is created and controlled by a *person,* one who thinks, speaks, acts rationally, loves and judges the world. To deny that God exists is to say that the world owes its ultimate origin and direction to *impersonal* objects or forces, such as matter, motion, time, and chance. But impersonal objects and forces cannot justify ethical obligations. A study of matter, motion, time, and chance will tell you what *is* up to a point, but it will not tell you what you *ought* to do. An impersonal universe imposes no absolute obligations.[27]

Frame continues his point with these words: "We cannot be obligated to atoms, or gravity, or evolution, or time, or chance; we can be obligated only to persons . . . An *absolute* standard, one without exceptions, one that binds everybody, must be based on loyalty to a person great enough to deserve such respect. Only God meets that description."[28]

There is no understanding of sin and forgiveness in the writings of Karl Marx, who reduced human evil to greed and a grasping for property. Marx's writings imply that the elimination of private property will lead to an abolishment of human evil. The falsity of this thesis is easily demonstrated by an examination of the behavior of the rulers of Marxist states.

Conclusion

A century and a half after the publication of *The Communist Manifesto*, it is difficult to find one substantial assertion in Marx's writings that has not been falsified. That so many intelligent people turn to Marxian ideology is a testimony to the power of worldviews to take control of people's lives and actions. In chapter 12, we will revisit the issue of Marxism and examine several new ways of interpreting Marx and the powerful influence these new systems are having on people in our generation.

For Further Reading

Isaiah Berlin, *Karl Marx* (New York: Oxford University Press, 1963).

M. M. Bober, *Karl Marx's Interpretation of History* (Cambridge, Mass.: Harvard University Press, 1948).

M. Cornforth, *Historical Materialism* (London: Lawrence & Wishart, 1953).

Louis Dupre, *The Philosophical Foundations of Marxism* (New York: Harcourt, Brace and World, 1966).

Sidney Hook, *From Hegel to Marx* (New York: John Day, 1950).

Sidney Hook, ed., *Marx and the Marxists* (Princeton, N.J.: D. Van Nostrand, 1955).

Sidney Hook, *Towards an Understanding of Karl Marx* (New York: John Day, 1933).

G. Lichtheim, *Marxism: An Historical and Critical Study* (New York: Praeger, 1961).

Karl Marx, *The Portable Karl Marx,* ed. Eugene Kamenka (New York: Penguin, 1983).

Karl Marx, *Karl Marx: A Reader*, ed. Jon Elster (New York: Cambridge University Press, 1986).

A. P. Mendel, ed., *Essential Works of Marxism* (New York: Bantam Books, 1961).

Melvin Rader, *Marx's Interpretation of History* (New York: Oxford University Press, 1979).

William H. Shaw, *Marx's Theory of History* (London: Hutchinson, 1978).

R. C. Tucker, *Philosophy and Myth in Karl Marx* (Cambridge, England: Cambridge University Press, 1961).

CHAPTER ELEVEN

SPENGLER AND TOYNBEE

Much has happened in the field of speculative history during the twentieth century. Spatial limitations make it necessary to restrict our comments to just two participants in this enterprise, namely, the German Oswald Spengler and the Englishman Arnold Toynbee.

Oswald Spengler

Oswald Spengler's (1880–1936) *The Decline of the West* was published in Germany in 1918. Before his book appeared, Spengler was an unknown mathematics teacher in Bavaria. The pessimistic conclusions of his book were so in tune with the mood of the day that he and his book quickly gained a wide hearing. The early influence of the book, however, could hardly be attributed to the content or style of the book, which was rambling, repetitious, and obscure.

Spengler advances principles that he claims are derived directly from history. These principles draw attention to basic similarities in the history of the major cultures of the world; they also make it possible for Spengler to predict the general course of future history. Spengler's prediction so far as Western culture is concerned is one of doom; even now, he maintains, we can see the beginning of the end. Spengler rejects the straight line pattern in favor of a biological analogy. He compares cultures to organisms, each having its own life cycle.

Spengler contrasts what he calls the Ptolemaic systems of history with his own Copernican approach. Ptolemaic systems of history assume that history should be interpreted from the standpoint of the historian's own perspective in Western culture. According to this view, the great cultures are made to follow orbits around us as the presumed center of all world happenings. Such histories, Spengler argues, suffer from being based upon a limited or incorrect point of reference. They ignore the whole process of history outside the sphere of Western influence. In opposition to this, Spengler's own "Copernican" approach to history admits no sort of privileged position to the Classical or Western culture as over against the cultures of India, Babylon, China, Egypt, the Arabs, or Mexico. There is not just one history whose supposed linear development leads inexorably and progressively to our own "modern" day. There are many histories of many cultures, each with its own ideas, life, will, feeling—and its own death.

According to Spengler, the basic units of history are cultures. Each culture is self-contained; there is no interdependence between them. The basic world concept for Greece and Rome, for example, was the atom; in our own age, it is infinity. This model symbolizes the modern confidence in unlimited horizons. The purpose of the philosophy of history is to set forth a "comparative morphology of cultures." Spengler tries to apply the biologist's concept of living forms to the basic cultures in history; he believes that each culture goes through a cycle similar to that of living organisms. Each of the eight fully developed cultures[1] has suffered through the same cycle of growth and decay. Cultures are born, grow strong, weaken, and die. Some live longer, some have been stronger, but all have ossified and fallen into a period of decadence and dissolution marked by commercialization and vulgarization.

Spengler teaches that every culture evolves through four stages that he compares to the four seasons and the major stages of a human life. In the first stage (the season of spring or the childhood of a human being), life is simple, lived largely on the basis of farming, although both mythology and religion appear on the scene. Spengler suggests that the spring of Western culture can be found during the Renaissance and Reformation. The second stage is analogous to the season of summer or human adolescence.

As summer is followed by autumn, so the autumn period of a culture marks the first signs of cultural decline. Nonetheless, we find the development of cities, the spread of commerce, the elevation of science and philosophy over religion, and growing signs of skepticism and revolution. In the case of Western culture, the period in question would include the Enlightenment.

The last stage is the winter of a culture, when the culture becomes a civilization. It is the season of deadly cold, advancing age, and death. In the last stage of a culture, quantity becomes more important than quality, utility more significant than beauty, and control passes to the merchants of war. The worldview becomes materialistic and people focus on science, wealth, and war.

Spengler's words certainly describe the West in his lifetime. In Spengler's mind, this justifies his claim that Western civilization is in its last period, hence his title *The Decline of the West.* Western civilization as seen in the states of Europe and America, the civilization that at his time dominated the planet, has reached and passed its peak. The decline has begun and death is inevitable.

Spengler draws an important distinction between cultures and civilizations. Cultures are young and full of life while civilizations are old, decrepit, and nearing death. Each culture has its own basic world concept, that is, a basic model or picture. Gordon Clark provides a helpful account of this part of Spengler's theory:

> Civilizations are the most external and artificial of all human productions. They are the rigidity that follows expansion and are the inevitable conclusion of life. The Greeks had a culture; the Romans had a civilization. The Romans were the unspiritual barbarians, devoid of art, intent on tangible success, who closed a period of culture. In the western world, as

Spengler views it, the transition from culture to civilization occurred in the nineteenth century.[2]

Once one recognizes the signs of advancing age, it is easier to make predictions about what may lie generally in the immediate future of a civilization. Since the West has passed into its civilization stage, we can be quite confident that the decline will continue until the inevitable arrival of its end.

Crucial to Spengler's analysis of Western culture is his view that events in different cultures and different ages can be "contemporaneous" with each other. For example, Napoleon was morphologically contemporaneous with Alexander the Great, while Hannibal was contemporaneous with World War I. In 1918, Spengler announced that the West was still awaiting its Julius Caesar.[3] Not only is this morphological principle helpful in predicting the future, it is an indispensable guide (providing one accepts it) for reconstructing the unknown past. It is difficult indeed to find any historians or philosophers who have found Spengler's morphological principle helpful.

Spengler's philosophy can be summed up in three words: Relativism, Pessimism, and Determinism. His relativism was a consequence of his views that history has no ultimate point of reference and that each culture is wholly self-contained. There are no abiding religious or moral ideas since all beliefs are relative to their respective culture. If this were true (and of course, given Spengler's relativism, even *his* positions cannot be true in the common sense of the word), it would mean that members of one culture would be unable to make value judgments about the actions and beliefs of people in other cultures. Spengler even went so far as to say a member of one culture could never understand the beliefs and ideals of any other culture. He was apparently unaware that this claim vitiated his own philosophy of history.

Objections

Spengler's failings are many. He seems unaware of the fallacious way in which he begins with his biological analogy and then, without an argument, leaps to the point where suddenly his readers are dealing with the supposed necessities of a presumed law of nature. His belief that humans are unable to act independently of their environment leads him to ignore important issues of human freedom and choice. Spengler elevates instinct and feeling above reason and principles. Moreover, his ideas helped create an environment in Germany that aided the Nazis' rise to power in the early 1930s.

Spengler's work grows dim in the light of the internal inconsistencies of his system and the later achievements of Arnold Toynbee. While we may be forced to agree with Spengler that Western culture is declining, we will have to assert this on grounds different from those he offered.

Arnold Toynbee

Arnold Toynbee's (1889–1975) *A Study of History* has been the most important and most widely discussed work in the philosophy of history since Hegel. The first three volumes of this mammoth study were published in 1934, the next three in 1939. Then a period of fifteen years elapsed until Toynbee published Volumes 7 through 10 in 1954. These four volumes revealed a marked shift in Toynbee's thought, a shift that will require some comment shortly. Two further volumes, the last entitled *Reconsiderations* (1964), completed the study.[4] As the title of the last volume suggests, Toynbee modified even more of his earlier claims in response to criticisms.

Toynbee and Spengler

Toynbee tells us that there were two formative influences that suggested his study to him. First, about the time World War I was beginning, he became aware of some remarkable similarities between the history of Greece-Rome and that of his own time. He began to wonder if there might be similar parallels elsewhere in history. Then at the end of the war, he came upon Spengler's *Decline of the West,* which tended to confirm his earlier suspicions. Toynbee was not satisfied with Spengler's work. He thought it was too limited in scope (Spengler had examined only eight civilizations), it paid too little attention to facts, it did not offer an adequate explanation of what brought about the rise and decline of new cultures, and it was too pessimistic. Toynbee was to make much of this last difference in his later writings. He contrasted the pessimistic determinism of Spengler with his own view that humans possess the power to change the course of the future and prevent the impending destruction of Western civilization.[5]

Toynbee was certainly right regarding this difference with Spengler. Spengler, as we have seen, was a determinist and a compulsive pessimist. Toynbee was far more optimistic about the future and came to reject deterministic views about the collapse of societies. This allowed Toynbee to express at least some measure of hope concerning the future of Western civilization.

Key Points in Toynbee's View of History

For Toynbee, the proper units of historical study are not nation-states or periods of time, but whole societies. Toynbee's units of history are larger than Spengler's, and he thinks he discovered more of them—twenty-one, in fact. Toynbee's purpose, at least in his first six volumes, was to study every known society to see if he could discover the factors that led to their rise and fall. His answer as to why civilizations rise is his doctrine of Challenge-and-Response. The first six civilizations arose out of primitive life by responding to challenges posed by their physical environment. For example, the civilization of Egypt was a response to the growing aridness of the Sahara Desert. Confronted by this challenge, the early Egyptians drained the marshes of the lower Nile. Thus their response to the challenge of their environment led to one of the great civilizations of world history. The challenges that confronted the fifteen civilizations that followed were less environmental and more along the line of threats of invasion or oppression. However, Toynbee explains, a challenge can sometimes be too easy or too severe. He traces a type of Golden Mean through history to show that challenges that are too easy do not invoke sufficient response, whereas challenges that are too harsh tend to stifle and smother any effective response. For example, Massachusetts posed its early settlers with a more severe challenge than South Carolina; its challenge was met by a more successful response. However, the challenge of Labrador was too severe and attempts at colonization there met with little success.

But how do we know when a civilization is growing? Is there any criterion of growth? The criterion Toynbee proposes is a special kind of change he calls etherialization. Civilizations grow by responding to a series of challenges. These challenges gradually become more spiritual in nature. As a society overcomes material obstacles and physical challenges, power is released which enables the society to respond to challenges which are internal and spiritual rather than external and material. Eventually, however, each past civilization reached a stage where it could not advance any higher.

Every civilization rises to a universal state in which there exists a unity of law, purpose, belief, and government. After the universal state is attained, the civilization begins to break up. Until now, the society has been led by a "creative minority," a small group of leaders who have led it during its period of growth and who have provided spiritual leadership for the masses ("the proletariat"). The creative minority gradually degenerates into a dominant minority. Even though the same leadership is still in control, it has become stagnant; it has lost its ability to inspire people to follow voluntarily and thus resorts to force. The turn towards coercion produces secessions from society on the part of those who earlier had been the uncreative majority.

Toynbee's uncreative majority includes people from two groups: the majority of people within the borders of the society who had followed the lead of the creative minority, along with the uncivilized people beyond the borders who had also followed the leaders. This secession and schism produces two proletariats that Toynbee called the internal and the external. In this way, then, the civilization becomes increasingly divided into three factions: the dominant minority, the internal proletariat,[6] and the external proletariat (barbarians beyond the authority of the dominant minority). Given this situation, a change in leadership is inevitable.

Three further steps followed. The uncreative minority that then controls the society by force produces a universal state; the dissatisfied internal proletariat helps give birth to a universal church; and the external proletariat generates war bands of barbarians.

What most good teachers would love to have at this point are specific illustrations from Toynbee to help students grasp his points. Regrettably, Toynbee offers no such help. The examples he does provide concern such arcane groups and events from periods of time so unknown to modern readers that they leave one suspecting he has stacked the deck in his favor and ignored other groups and events that would weaken his thesis. One can search his volumes in vain for illuminating examples from Western civilization that would be helpful to readers at the end of the twentieth century.

Societies break down then, when, because of a lack of creative leadership, they become unable to respond to further challenges. The breakdowns in civilizations never spring from external causes but from inherent defects in humans themselves.

Toynbee ends Volume 6 of his work by holding out the hope that if modern people return to God, there is still a chance that Western civilization might be saved. In Toynbee's words, "We may and must pray that a reprieve which God has granted to our society once will not be refused if we ask for it again in a contrite spirit and with a broken heart."[7]

Toynbee's Change of Mind

Toynbee's 1934 volumes argued for a cyclical pattern of history. He contended that when any of history's civilizations collapsed, they were followed by the rise of what he called a universal state, a universal church, and barbarians outside of the bounds of that civilization.[8] By the time his 1939 volumes appeared, the belief that history is nothing but an eternally repeating circle had become unacceptable to Toynbee. He then suggests that each cycle in history might produce new developments. In his words, "The perpetual turning of a wheel is not a vain repetition if, at each revolution, it is carrying a vehicle that much nearer its goal."[9] The instrument of this new result is the series of universal churches that bridges civilizations.[10] Still more changes appear in his 1954 volumes when he makes civilizations subordinate to the universal churches.[11] As civilizations deteriorate, religions are born out of the suffering.[12] Human knowledge of God grows as civilizations collapse. In his last volume, Toynbee makes clear his skepticism about offering predictions, especially where the future of the West is concerned.[13] It is true, he writes, that

> I think that a pattern of breakdown and disintegration, common to the histories of a number of past civilizations, can be detected when we make a comparative study of them. But I do not believe that this pattern was predetermined or inevitable in any single past case; and therefore, *a fortiori*, I do not believe, as Spengler believes, that there is a fixed pattern to which the history of every civilization is bound to conform. My unwillingness to predict that the Western Civilization will go the way that a number of its predecessors have gone is a consistent application of my conviction that the course of human affairs is not predetermined.[14]

Toynbee admits that because the development of Western civilization is still incomplete, he does not believe anyone can predict its future. In fact, he admits, it is so young that it may not even be possible to identify the pattern of its past. "There is room for many patterns; they are not mutually exclusive."[15]

Toynbee's Changing View of Religion

Read superficially, it seemed to many readers that Toynbee was touting Christianity, something that could hardly have been the case because of Toynbee's denial that any religion possesses the final truth. What happened during Toynbee's odyssey was that he abandoned his earlier cyclical understanding of history in favor of a more linear view resembling the historic Christian theory, with the result that he ended up with a kind of spiral theory.[16] History, Toynbee came to believe, was advancing towards a goal, but it was not the goal described in the Christian Scriptures. Toynbee's goal was a syncretistic religion.

In this way, Toynbee quietly abandoned many of his earlier views and came to argue that the ultimate goal of history is a new religious society based upon a universal church that would combine elements of the world's major religions. According to the later Toynbee, the evolution of religion has produced the four higher religions[17] that dominate the modern world. None of these religions, he believed, is the product of divine revelation; rather, all of them are only the manifestation of fundamental psychological needs. In Volume 12, Toynbee defines the "higher religions" as "religions designed to bring human beings into direct communion with absolute spiritual Reality as individuals, in contrast to earlier forms of religion that have brought them only into indirect communion with it through the medium of the particular society in which they have happened to be participants."[18]

He then explains that his so-called "universal churches" are universal, "not in the literal meaning of the word, but in the belief and expectation of their adherents. They have been the institutional vehicles of missionary religions whose exponents have set out to convert the whole of mankind."[19] Toynbee's view of universal churches is modified considerably in Volumes 7 to 10. In the first six volumes, the more important units of historical investigation were civilizations. But in the later volumes, the universal churches assume much more prominence, as Toynbee lost interest in civilizations as the basic unity of historical study. Civilizations in his new approach were said to exist in order to promote the development of religion.

Toynbee hoped the Western world would become more open to a syncretistic faith. The only significant element of Christianity to be preserved in this new faith is its emphasis on the love of God. Toynbee's projected new religion rejects any exclusivist element of traditional Christianity, including all of its doctrines. It includes the kind of alleged "tolerance" toward doctrinal deviation more often found in the religions of the East.[20]

The later Toynbee has little use for the essential elements of historic Christianity, such as divine special revelation, miracles, and prophecy. His substitute religion reflects the religious liberalism of his time. Religion, he believed, is grounded not on special revelation but upon evolving human experience.

Some Objections

Toynbee's critics were often merciless in attacking his failings, such as his propensity towards oversimplification and his alleged ignorance of important literature.[21] The fact that many of their objections hit home is evident in Toynbee's acknowledgments in Volume 12 of his work.

Well-known British author and Roman Catholic layman Christopher Dawson describes Toynbee's radical change of mind in Volumes 6 through 10 as a "fundamental modification of his earlier views and involves the transformation of his *Study of History* from a relativist phenomenology of equivalent cultures, after the fashion of Spengler, into a unitary philosophy of history comparable to that of the idealist philosophers of the nineteenth century."[22] This change, Dawson argues,

> marks the abandonment of his original theory of the philosophical equivalence of the civilizations and the introduction of a qualitative principle embodied in the Higher Religions which are regarded as representative of a higher species of society, and which stand in the same relation to the civilizations as the latter to the primitive societies. Thus Toynbee's theory of history ceases to be cyclical, like Spengler's, and becomes a progressive series of four world stages ascending from primitive societies, through the primary and secondary civilizations to the higher religions in which history finds its ultimate goal.[23]

It is commendable that a scholar of Toynbee's stature would admit some of his errors and change his position. Nonetheless, what we are left with at the end of Volume 12 amounts to a repudiation of many of the essential features of Toynbee's early work that brought him international recognition. Many who read Toynbee's later volumes did so because of the way Western culture creates intellectual icons. They did not understand that what they were reading in the newer volumes was effectively a repudiation of the system of Volumes 1 through 3 that had made Toynbee famous in the first place.

Finally, some criticism must be directed at Toynbee's inadequate, distorted, and biased view of the historic Christian faith. His failure to understand the faith of his early years, even though of a quite liberal variety, compromises seriously his eventual attack upon that faith. It also helps us understand why the change in worldviews blinded him to the impossibility of producing a synthesis of the contradictory beliefs of the other so-called universal churches.[24]

Final Comments

Even though it is still necessary for surveys of the philosophy of history to discuss their work, the writings of Spengler and Toynbee are now curios of an earlier time in this century. Such expressions as "Time marches on" and "As the world turns" come to mind as one reflects on how quickly the work of authors like Spengler and Toynbee can drop out of sight.

For Further Reading About Spengler

Christopher Dawson, *The Dynamics of World History,* ed. John J. Mulloy, (La Salle, Ill.: Sherwood Sugden & Co., 1978).

Klaus Fischer, *History and Prophecy: Oswald Spengler and the Decline of the West* (New York: P. Lang, 1989).

E. H. Goddard and P. A. Gibbons, *Civilization or Civilizations: An Essay in the Spenglerian Philosophy of History* (London: Constable, 1926).

H. Stewart Hughes, *Oswald Spengler: A Critical Analysis* (New Brunswick, N.J.: Transaction Publishers, 1991).

Bruce Mazlish, *The Riddle of History* (New York: Harper and Row, 1966).

John J. Reilly, *Spengler's Future* (New Brunswick, N.J.: Millennium, 1993).

Oswald Spengler, *The Decline of the West,* tr. C. F. Atkinson (New York: Alfred A. Knopf, 1928).

For Further Reading About Toynbee

Edward Gargan, ed. *The Intent of Toynbee's History* (Chicago: Loyola University Press, 1961).

Peter Geyl, Arnold Toynbee, and Pitirim A. Sorokin, *The Pattern of the Past: Can We Determine It?* (Boston: Beacon Press, 1949).

H. L. Mason, *Toynbee's Approach to World Politics* (New Orleans: Tulane University Press, 1958).

C. T. McIntire and Marvin Perry, eds., *Toynbee: A Reappraisal* (Toronto: University of Toronto Press, 1996).

Robert Paul Mohan, *Philosophy of History: An Introduction* (New York: Bruce Publishing Co., 1970).

F. M. Ashley Montague, ed., *Toynbee and History: Critical Essays and Reviews* (New York: Porter Sargant, 1956).

Marvin Perry, *Arnold Toynbee and the Western Tradition* (New York: Peter Lang, 1996).

Pitirim Sorokin, "Toynbee's Philosophy of History," in *The Journal of Modern History*, Vol. 12 (1940), 374–87.

Pitirim Sorokin, "Toynbee's Study of History: The Last Four Volumes," in *The Annals of the American Academy of Political and Social Sciences*, Vol. 299 (May, 1955), 144–46.

C. Gregg Singer, *Toynbee* (Nutley, N.J.: Presbyterian and Reformed, 1977).

Arnold Toynbee, *A Study of History*, 12 volumes (New York: Oxford University Press, 1936–1964.

CHAPTER TWELVE

THE NEW FACE OF MARXISM

If this book contained a chapter on every interpretation of Karl Marx published in the last century, there would be room for nothing else. Many of the newer variety of Marxian interpreters, however, allege that the views presented in chapter 10 are outdated. Some Marxists hold such an exalted view of Marx that they oppose any suggestion that he was wrong about anything, with the possible exception of his personal brand of toothpaste. It has been true that whenever Marx *is* proven wrong on some issue, his defenders jump into the breach and attempt to rescue Marx's writings from the junk pile of history. One way this is done is by claiming it is not Marx who is wrong but his incompetent interpreters who do not know how to read him. The exposition of the classical Marx in the previous chapter, however, is neither outdated nor inaccurate. It is important that future generations understand thoroughly what Marx believed and taught.

A second reason why this chapter is necessary is because the new forms of Marxism represent a quite different approach to history than anything else covered in this book. A book about the meaning of history dare not ignore the new challenge posed by these revisions of the classical Marx.

The approach to Marx discussed in this chapter has several different names. It is sometimes called *Neo-Marxism*, an obvious code word for what is supposed to be a new stage in Marxian thinking. Elements of Neo-Marxism are often referred to as *Humanistic Marxism*, for reasons that will be explained shortly. It is also known as *Western Marxism,* because it originated after 1930 in the thinking of a group of German Marxists who came to be known as the Frankfurt School, a name that understandably grew out of their association with the Institute of Social Research in Frankfurt, Germany.

The best-known representative of the Frankfurt School became the philosopher Herbert Marcuse, about whom much will be said in this chapter. Over time, a small number of thinkers from other nations have been added to the Neo-Marxist pantheon. Today the best-known representative of this non-German group is the Italian communist Antonio Gramsci.

Neo-Marxism has had a significant impact on many so-called liberation theologians.[1] Leading liberationists have attempted to bring about a synthesis of what they still call Christianity and Marxism. Major elements of Neo-Marxism have been present for years in the thinking, teaching, and writings of many American college professors, including some in evangelical colleges and seminaries. Several writings of evangelical sociologist Tony Campolo reflect this influence.[2]

Neo-Marxism has proven very resilient over the last thirty years, even though signs of its inevitable collapse are obvious. In fact, one 1989 book states that "the Frankfurt School, in its original form, and as a school of Marxism or sociology, is dead."[3] This claim, however, must be taken with some caution. While the old Frankfurt School *is* dead, the radical ideas of Herbert Marcuse and Antonio Gramsci continue to thrive in the hearts and minds of many American university professors who were part of the New Left movement twenty-five to thirty years ago.[4] As these unrepentant radicals continue to win converts among their current students, new spins on older Marxist theories continue to develop.

The neo-Marxist view of history differs from what we found in classical Marxism. When one gets beyond the necessary place of revolution in the classical Marx, his system was a peculiar variety of the progress dogma. In contrast, neo-Marxists tend to be pessimists who reject progress as a delusion.

Neo-Marxism and Herbert Marcuse

Leading members of the Institute for Social Research in Frankfurt, Germany (mentioned above), fled Nazi Germany in 1933, eventually reaching the United States. One of these individuals was Herbert Marcuse (1898–1979), who had studied philosophy at the universities of Berlin and Freiberg and joined the Institute in 1932. The Institute remained in the U.S. until 1950 when most of its members, Marcuse being a notable exception, returned to Frankfurt.[5] During World War II, Marcuse worked for the Office of Strategic Services (OSS), the forerunner to today's Central Intelligence Agency (CIA). It is unlikely that more than a few of Marcuse's adoring followers in the radical Left fully understood his relationship to the spy agency they detested. But perhaps they would not have cared, since Marcuse used his connections to help Marxist allies gain positions of influence and power in the postwar German government.

Marcuse taught philosophy at Columbia and Brandeis Universities, and after 1967 at the University of California at San Diego, where he became an icon to student radicals in the New Left movement. One book describes Marcuse's fame among American radicals as follows: "When students recently [1968] forced the closing of the University of Rome . . . they carried a banner inscribed with three M's. The initials stood for a new triumvirate: Marx, Mao and Marcuse. To thousands of young people, Marx is the prophet, Mao the sword, and Marcuse the ideological spokesman of the radical New Left."[6]

Marcuse's so-called humanistic interpretation of Marx differs from other forms of Marxism in terms of the importance it attaches to a number of Marx's early unpublished manuscripts.[7] Three things should be noted about these early writings. (1) Marx made no effort to publish them, surely a surprising fact about material that is supposed to capture the heart and soul of his system. (2) Marx wrote these early manuscripts four years before he and Engels published the *Manifesto of the Communist Party* in 1848. In the opinion of many Marxist scholars, this means Marx wrote these early manuscripts before he himself even became a Marxist! (3) The early manuscripts were not published (in German) until 1932. Publication of English translations would come years later.

The most important doctrine contained in the early manuscripts is Marx's teaching about human alienation, a point that helps to explain why the view is sometimes called "Humanistic Marxism." Marx is thought to have identified four different but related forms of worker alienation. First, capitalism supposedly causes workers to become alienated from that which they produce. Because the capitalist system creates false needs and provides false satisfactions, workers are manipulated into wanting things and then seduced into buying them. Workers become dominated and controlled by the things they are forced to make.

Second, workers are estranged from the labor process itself. Of course, it takes little effort to note how many men and women hate their jobs. This alienation is not restricted to those who must labor at menial, repetitive, boring, dirty, or degrading tasks. Even professional golfers and philosophers have been known to hold an occasional loathing for their jobs.

Third, workers under capitalism allegedly become alienated from other men and women, a fact easily observed by noting the widespread competitiveness, hostility, and animosity among human beings. Proponents of the humanistic version of Marx want us to believe that all manifestations of these traits in the modern world are consequences of capitalism.

In the fourth kind of alienation, workers not only become alienated from what they produce, from their work, and from other workers; finally they become alienated from themselves.

Any of these forms of alienation is serious enough to warrant concern. But the important question becomes to what extent Marx should be given credit for discovering the problem and recommending a solution. For one thing, the theory of alienation is neither unique to Marx nor original with him. It can be found in a number of thinkers before Marx, and it was developed independently by several writers after Marx. Moreover, human alienation is hardly unique to capitalist societies. It is difficult to believe that garbage collectors in Moscow are any happier with their jobs than garbage collectors in Boston, Cleveland, or Beverly Hills. Alienation and dehumanization are serious problems, but it simply is not true that they result exclusively from conditions existing in capitalist societies and vanish once those societies have become socialist.[8] Human alienation is no more an exclusive effect of capitalism than baldness.

The development of Neo-Marxism obviously had to await the publication of Marx's early writings, an event that took place in 1932. In the early 1930s, the early manuscripts seemed to reveal a Marx quite different from the official Marx of Soviet Stalinism. For people weary of or frightened by the ruthless tyranny of Joseph Stalin, Marx's newly discovered writings made it possible to appeal to the authority of the early Marx in defense of individual human dignity and freedom, or so some people claimed.

The appearance of anti-Stalinist attitudes and the gradual rejection of Marxism-Leninism among a number of Communists in Eastern Europe after World War II added to the appeal of the humanistic interpretation. As Sidney Hook explains,

> Aware that they could only get a hearing or exercise influence if they spoke in the name of Marxism, [such non-Leninists] seized upon several formulations in these early manuscripts of Marx in which he glorifies the nature of man as a freedom-loving creature—a nature that has been distorted, cramped, and twisted by the capitalist mode of production. They were then able to protest in the name of Marxist humanism against the stifling dictatorship of Stalin and his lieutenants in their own countries, and even against the apotheosis of Lenin.[9]

In other words, the Stalinist contempt for human rights gave added incentive to some Marxists to find a new Marx whose name and authority could be used to bring about a restoration of humanitarian concerns in the brutal conditions that prevailed under Stalin.

A number of people in Western Europe took these appeals to the early Marx seriously and began to claim that the humanistic version of Marx was what Marxism should always have been. Marx's early teaching about human nature and alienation was presented as the essence of the socialism taught in Marx's later writings. The goal of Marx's socialism in this new interpretation was the emancipation of humans from all that would deny their essential humanity. So what began in Eastern Europe as an attempt to find an acceptable basis for humanism within a Marxist context became in the West a new way of glorifying Marx for those seeking his authority for their own causes. Daniel Bell finds it remarkable that "a whole school of neo-Marxists . . . has gone back to the early doctrines of alienation in order to find the basis for a new, humanistic interpretation of Marx."[10]

In this new view, Sidney Hook writes:

> Marxism is not primarily a system of sociology or economics, but a philosophy of human liberation. It seeks to overcome human alienation, to emancipate man from repressive social institutions, especially economic institutions that frustrate his true nature, and to bring him into harmony with himself, his fellow men, and the world around him so that he can both overcome his estrangements and express his true essence through creative freedom.[11]

In this way, a Marxist message came into existence that is an alternative to the totalitarian terror of Lenin's Bolshevism.

As we will see, there are two fatal flaws in Neo-Marxism. First, Neo-Marxism depends on an utterly untenable reading of Marx's writings. Second, the developers of Neo-Marxism advocated their own kind of totalitarianism.

Problems with the Humanistic Interpretation of Marx

When the humanistic interpretation first appeared in the early 1930s, old-style Leninists and Stalinists were taken off guard. Early proponents of the view who had the misfortune of being where Joseph Stalin could get his hands on them were given two choices (even though they were not fully informed about the end result). Either they were forced to recant publicly, or they simply disappeared. In either case, the usual result was a bullet in the brain.

The plausibility of Neo-Marxism depends to a great extent on the place Marx's early unpublished writings should have in any correct understanding of his system. Neo-Marxists insist that Marx's later writings should be interpreted in light of the early writings. According to Erich Fromm, "It is impossible to understand Marx's concept of socialism and his criticism of capitalism as developed except on the basis of his concept of man which he developed in his early writings."[12] Neo-Marxists believe Marx's position remained basically the same from his early 1844 writings through his later publications. The clue that supposedly reveals the meaning of the entire system lies hidden in the early unpublished manuscripts. Neo-Marxists largely ignore the teachings for which Marx became most famous, namely, the labor theory of value, dialectical materialism, and the class struggle. Under the new view, Marx is a philosopher whose primary concern is to draw attention to human estrangement caused by an oppressive society. As noted earlier, this assumption grounds one of the labels of the theory, Humanistic Marxism.

Critics of Neo-Marxism have tended to dismiss both the early writings and their teaching about alienation, denying that they are essential to the real Marx. Many of these critics believe that the early and later writings contain two different and incompatible systems. These critics argue that the supposed humanism of the early Marx is simply not germane to the concerns of the later Marx. Sidney Hook expresses his amazement this way: "The most fantastic interpretations have been placed on these [early] groping efforts of Marx towards intellectual maturity."[13]

One jarring consequence of the Neo-Marxist reading of Marx is its implication that no one really understood Marx until the day in 1932 when his early writings on alienation and related topics were finally published. Serious scholars know that later in life, Marx abandoned the rambling comments about human alienation in his unpublished manuscripts; his mature writings are incompatible with Neo-Marxist dogma.[14] The early Marx saw private property as an effect of alienation. In his later writings, however, he treated private property as the cause of the alienation that had been so important to him in the 1844 manuscripts. The two positions are totally inconsistent.

Marx devoted twenty years of hard labor to his book *Capital*; it was a book for which he sacrificed almost everything in his life including health and family. Nonetheless, the humanistic version of Marx turns *Capital*, in the words of Robert Tucker, into "an intellectual museum piece . . . whereas the sixteen-page manuscript of 1844 on the future of aesthetics, which he probably wrote in a day and never even saw fit to publish, contains much that is still significant."[15] To make things even worse, the mature Marx actually repudiated his early doctrine of alienation.[16] All of this becomes especially ironic for devotees of liberation theology and their attempt to integrate a heterodoxical version of Christianity with Humanistic Marxism. As the information in this section shows, their efforts rest on a questionable interpretation of questionable writings that are the basis of a questionable theory that, in all likelihood, Marx himself repudiated. The Christian use of Marxism in liberation theology, it appears, is a system built on quicksand.[17]

Neo-Marxist Totalitarianism

Herbert Marcuse was a severe critic of all advanced industrial societies, especially the United States. While Marx believed that workers would carry the revolution, Marcuse thought Marx failed to see how the workers would eventually become part of the establishment. According to Marcuse, the workers in advanced industrial societies become corrupted by the affluence of their society until they have the same values as the oppressor class.

Marcuse taught that modern technology in Western societies eliminates dissent that might arise in less advanced societies by creating false needs and providing false satisfaction. Such technology enslaves people by deceiving them into thinking that it gives them what they really want: better homes and appliances, faster cars, more leisure and luxury. In effect, Americans are so completely dominated, controlled, preconditioned, indoctrinated, and brainwashed that they cannot even recognize their bondage. Tom Bottomore summarizes Marcuse's position:

> The two main classes in capitalist society—bourgeoisie and proletariat—have disappeared as effective historical agents; hence there is, on one side, no dominant *class*, but instead domination by an impersonal power ("scientific-technological rationality") and on the other side, no opposing *class*, for the

> working class has been assimilated and pacified, not only through high mass consumption but in the rationalized process of production itself.[18]

By the time Marcuse was finished making his case, it seemed impossible that anyone in any advanced industrial society might rebel against the hand that feeds him.

Marcuse attacked this false mass contentment by claiming that the goods produced by capitalism provide false satisfaction. First the system manipulates people into wanting things; then it seduces them into buying them; and, through devices like advertising, it increases these wants until the desire to consume becomes compulsive and irrational. The belief of average people that they are happy only shows how total their bondage is. The things that make us think we are happy (electric can openers, indoor toilets, diet colas, boysenberry-flavored breakfast cereals) are the chains that bind us. Marcuse *knew* the members of a capitalist society were really unhappy. Marcuse knew their needs were the false products of a repressive society. What we really need, he claimed, is to free ourselves from false consciousness and its artificial needs and gain true consciousness and its recognition of true needs. We need to become a new type of human being that cannot be seduced by affluence.

It was not enough, however, for Marcuse to argue that humans must free themselves from the oppressive influence of false needs imposed by a repressive society; he should also have explained *how* this could be done. As Marcuse himself puts it, "How can the people who have been the object of effective and productive domination by themselves create the conditions of freedom?"[19] Marcuse may have backed himself into a corner with no way out. He has placed humanity in such a sealed box that the attainment of the autonomy and liberation he hoped for is impossible. After all, he himself had said that because it was impossible for those dominated by the system ever to free themselves from it, there is no way for the system to correct itself.

But Marcuse was not finished; he went on to make things even more hopeless by claiming that social change could not take place through democratic means. This is so because democracy contributes to the plight of society by lulling people into decisions that are against their best interests. Look at who Americans elect as president, he could easily have added. Advanced industrial societies like the United States appear tolerant of minority views because they know that those views can have no effect. People are not really free when they vote and make political decisions because, according to Marcuse, all who start out under the domination of a repressive society are preconditioned receptacles; they are incapable of criticizing the society or even of heeding a legitimate criticism.

This led Marcuse to his doctrine of "Repressive Tolerance."[20] Because American society is in such peril, he came to believe that the suspension of free speech and free assembly are justified. After all, there is no real value to freedom of speech; it only insures the propagation of lies. Truth is carried by revolutionary minorities like Marcuse's disciples! Therefore, tolerance should be withdrawn from all who disagree with Marcuse and extended only to those who make what he called "the Great Refusal." Social change can be brought about not by democratic legality but by extra-democratic rebellion. Even though Marcuse wanted to replace democratically elected elites with an elite of his own choosing, he admitted that even if his totalitarian measures were put into practice and his followers succeeded in destroying existing society, he could not be sure what would follow.[21] As we will see shortly, many Marxists in the academic world also admit they have no idea what might follow the fulfillment of their dreams. But since they would then be in power, and since they are better people than the rest of us, we should feel at peace turning power over to them.

The questions raised by Marcuse's theory are obvious: How does his elite free itself from the conditioning that blinds everyone else? And who will provide deliverance from the repressiveness of his elite? Such considerations have led several interpreters of Marcuse to see signs of a neo-Nazi mentality in his position.[22]

While the first difficulty Marcuse saw in achieving liberation was the failure of the democratic process, the second was the powerlessness of critical social theory to criticize. The very categories of critical theory were developed within the structure of the system. Furthermore, those who might offer the criticism are preconditioned by the system. And finally, those who might otherwise be influenced by a criticism of their society are so brainwashed that they cannot appreciate the force of or understand the nature of the criticism. Thus, there is no one to offer the critique, no one to understand it, and no critical theory in terms of which the needed critique can be given. Things indeed look hopeless. But for whom? Perhaps Marcuse created a greater problem for himself than for capitalism.

Just when things looked hopeless, Marcuse, who wrote in the 1960s, began to see signs of "the Great Refusal" all over the place: the revolutions in Vietnam, Cuba, and China (of course, these Marxist-Leninist strongholds were hardly bastions of Neo-Marxism); guerrilla activities in Latin America: strains in the fortress of corporate capitalism; stirrings among ghetto populations; and, last but not least, student uprisings. He became both a prophet and a hero to the radical Left on America's college campuses.

But there was a huge and embarrassing hole right in the middle of Marcuse's argument. How, given the total domination of the repressive society, was all this opposition possible? Marcuse had claimed that *all* people living in advanced industrial societies are controlled, manipulated, and brainwashed to the extent that they think they are happy, are unable to see their society's faults, and are unable to appreciate criticisms of their society. The problem is that *Marcuse's thesis turns out to be self-defeating.* Why? Because no one, including Marcuse himself, could have obtained knowledge of the thesis! Even granting that his books could be the result of some kind of miracle, no one else, according to his theory, could have understood him.[23]

One more thing needs to be noted: Marcuse had little use for arguments or empirical evidence when it came to his system. In place of such, he urged people simply to watch television or listen to the radio for a few days, paying special attention to the commercials.

Marcuse's theory continues to exercise a bizarre hold over many academicians in the United States, including growing numbers of people who teach at evangelical colleges and seminaries or otherwise provide leadership for evangelical institutions.[24] It continues to be one of the mysteries of late twentieth-century thought how so many intellectuals can be so uncritically captive to a logically self-defeating set of ideas that turn out to lead in a totalitarian direction.

Neo-Marxism and History

For all of its faults, classical Marxism offered an understandable pattern of history, one that taught that history would continue to progress towards a classless society and the utopia that supposedly would follow. But the Neo-Marxists and others who pursue related ideologies claim that the Marxian view of the past and future as described in chapter 10 is a distortion of Marx's real beliefs. As this chapter has shown, the world still awaits a demonstration of that claim. The Neo-Marxists who denigrate classical Marxism have nothing to offer but the promise that those who miraculously understand the Neo-Marxist critique of Western society may safely place their blind trust in the Neo-Marxist intellectuals, join the revolution (whatever it means), and hope for the best.

One of the best accounts of this newer version of Marxism is presented by Lee Congdon, a professor of history at James Madison University. Congdon relates that when he was doing graduate work in history during the late sixties and early seventies, the teachers and students in the circles in which he traveled took Marxism very seriously. "Most history courses," he writes, "were taught from a Marxist, or a 'radical,' perspective and discussions in and out of class were punctuated with buzz words such as 'fascists,' 'ruling class,' 'liberation,' and that old stand-by 'the People.'"[25] For many of the Marxist professors and students, Congdon continues, "Marxism meant little more than a festering discontent and a rage that seemed to be greatest when it was least explicable. Only a handful of the more intelligent, and earnest, radicals ever bothered to read Marx."[26] Most of the Marxists in Congdon's university experience preferred the kind of Neo-Marxism explained earlier in this chapter.

Congdon reports that a helpful key to unlocking what really goes on in the minds of Marxist academicians can be found in the work of Antonio Gramsci (1891–1937), a founder of the Italian Communist Party, whose ideas are now regarded as representative of the new Western Marxism.[27] In 1928, at the age of 37, Gramsci was sentenced to prison for his political activities; he died in 1937, shortly after being released.

In Gramsci's view of the world, Marxists should not expect the final victory of socialism in the short term. If the radicals cannot have their revolution today, they can at least derive comfort from the knowledge that they can help lay the foundation for one in the more distant future. Since the workers in Gramsci's theory would not attain political power until they achieved intellectual control, academicians had a vital role to play after all. Gramsci's kind of Marxism made intellectuals, not workers, the primary force behind the revolution. What was most important in Gramsci's thinking was not economics but the culture.[28]

Gramsci developed a distinctively different theory about the societal role that intellectuals could play in helping to advance the Marxist cause. Marx had taught that the place of men and women in society shapes their consciousness. Gramsci believed human consciousness is shaped through what he called *hegemony*, which means intellectual and moral leadership.

Lee Congdon unpacks the implications of Gramsci's position for university communities:

> Thanks to Gramsci, then, radical intellectuals could have their cake and eat it. With a clear conscience, they could accept academic appointments at bourgeois institutions and still perform revolutionary acts, namely teaching, writing, and the making of a Marxist culture. That, certainly, is how Frederick Jameson, the extravagantly praised literary theorist sees it: "To create a Marxist culture in this country," he has written, "to make Marxism an unavoidable presence and a distinct, original, and unmistakable voice in American social, cultural and intellectual life, in short to form a Marxist intelligentsia for the struggles for the future—this seems to me the supreme mission of a Marxist pedagogy and a radical intellectual life today."[29]

Jameson's words seem to remove any doubt about what Marxist academicians in the West are really up to and how they view their work in the college classroom. The new Marxist culture which these radicals seek to bring about is to be "a culture of critical discourse," which means that it will be "negative through and through, at war with a culture that places a premium on received truths and hence . . . on a class authority hostile to non-conforming intellectuals."[30] What all of this means is that today's radical intellectuals have the critical task of organizing and training society. They must help to create a new way of life and a new worldview; they must help all the inferior members of society (everyone other than themselves) to appropriate *their* interests and values.

The army of professors and their student converts who make up this adversary culture is bent on separating us from our past by obliterating the past from our memory and rewriting history. The radical Left sees the function of education to be the nihilistic rejection of truth. Its purpose is to make students so dissatisfied that they will deny any value to anything except their version of Marxism. This means that in the process, they will work to subvert all of society, including institutions of higher learning. Marxist professors of this type believe they must find a way to take control of history. As Congdon explains, such radicals reason that if "they are to control the future, they must first take possession of the past by inducing selective amnesia and reinterpreting events in such a way as to promote contemporary political ambitions."[31]

The ambition of Marxist regimes has always been to possess and control human memory. Since our past helps to define who and what we are, control of what people remember of the past produces control of those people. This is why radical historians are so interested in rewriting the past in Marxist categories.

Why did so many college-educated people in the 1970s and 1980s believe that anti-communism is simplistic, just another hangover of the Cold War? Why did so many view the United States and the Soviet Union as morally equivalent? Why were so many Americans more critical of their own nation than of terrorist states abroad? It is difficult to ignore the indoctrination on behalf of these views that has become such an important message of left-wing academics. As the leftist influence on university communities has grown, it has become increasingly more difficult to keep education separated from ideological, political considerations. The reason is because the Left sees the propagation of its ideology as the primary objective of its educational activity.

> In view of Marxism's influence and increasingly nihilistic character, the guardianship and development of our tradition that are the humanities' principal responsibilities have taken on a fresh urgency. Those tasks are, in fact, far more consequential than efforts to promote public policy initiatives, however worthy they might be. If the tradition that bears our values is destroyed, we will lose hold of our very identity as individuals and as a people. If we allow the nihilistic impulse to go unchecked, we will put civilization itself at risk, with what consequences we ought by now to know.[32]

What these words provide is a new blueprint for revolution. It is obvious that the agents of revolution who follow these instructions will be willing, if necessary, to twist and deny the truth, to knowingly replace truth with lies, all in the service of seducing students and others into the new Marxist worldview.

Gramsci's new kind of revolution is a form of worldview indoctrination. According to Congdon, Marxist academicians who follow Gramsci view their university work differently than anything we have seen outside of totalitarian states such as Nazi Germany, the Soviet Union, Communist China, or Castro's Cuba. They see themselves as revolutionaries who must use their classroom teaching, their publishing, their work in hiring and firing faculty and administrators, and their work in curriculum revision as means to advancing the cause of their Marxist agenda. Lying at the very heart of Gramsci's vision of the new intellectual is the manipulation of truth and perceptions.[33]

Conclusion

Our examination of what are generally regarded as the most important approaches to speculative history is now over. As far as the problematic secular patterns of history are concerned, they make the Christian philosophy of history look attractive. When we dig even deeper and check the larger conceptual systems of which the secular theories are a part, things appear even more problematic. But, of course, all of us are different. In the final analysis, each will have to decide if any of the systems we've studied is a plausible and coherent alternative to the Christian worldview and its approach to history.

I must admit being mystified as to why anyone would look beyond the straight-line pattern that had its source in the Judeo-Christian revelation. The selection of Christianity's linear view, which inspired many of the secular theories anyway, appears to be the correct way to go. Secularists, as expected, will disapprove of what gets the line started (creation), and what lies at the end of the line (divine judgment), but that is another worldview issue. Naturalists have no way of explaining "beginnings," which is why they have to believe that "the box" has always existed. And when secularists begin to offer their predictions about the future, then it is time to run for the hills. None of the secular theories offers anything upon which wise men and women can rest their hope for the future.

And let us not forget the very troubling content of this last chapter. The objective of many neo-Marxist academicians, those who follow Gramsci's agenda, is to negate the nature of history, to change our understanding of the past, and to undermine the foundations of legitimate education in nations that have previously been independent of totalitarian impulses. As our investigation of speculative systems of history comes to an end, we find that many who today masquerade as guardians of the past are in fact enemies of scientific history. Thirty years ago, who would have thought that any historians in the West, regardless of ideology, would adopt a position that would reject scientific history in favor of propaganda?

I have spent much time in this book arguing for the importance of a worldview orientation in our approach to speculative systems of history. It is no secret, I guess, that I believe a fair appraisal of the worldview options in this area of human inquiry reveals that the much maligned and frequently misrepresented Christian worldview and its approach to history deserves a new look. If nothing else, it offers a perspective upon which a critique of the secular systems can be grounded. According to Gordon Clark, the choice of any of the secular systems leads to a setting in which

> history has no significance; human hopes are to be swallowed up in oblivion; and all men, good, evil, and indifferent, come to the same end. Anyone who chooses this view must base his life on unyielding despair. If however, he chooses

> the Christian view, then he can assign significance to history; human hopes and fears in this life contribute to the quality of a life after death, when two types of men will receive their separate destinies. Anyone who chooses this [Christian] view can look at the calamities of western civilization and say, "We know that all things work together for good to them that love God." There has been no proof, but there is a choice.[34]

While many, including this author, may believe there are good arguments to guide us in such a choice, Clark seems quite right in pointing his readers in the direction of the Christian view of history.

For Further Reading

Daniel Bell, *The End of Ideology* (New York: Free Press, 1960).

Robert S. Dombroski, *Antonio Gramsci* (Boston: Twayne Publishers, 1989).

Benedetto Fontana, *Hegemony and Power: On the Relation between Gramsci and Machiavelli* (Minneapolis: University of Minnesota Press, 1993).

Antonio Gramsci, *Letters from Prison,* selected, translated, and introduced by Lynne Lawner (New York: Harper & Row, 1973).

Renate Holub, *Antonio Gramsci: Beyond Marxism and Postmodernism* (London: Routledge, 1992).

Sidney Hook, *Marxism and Beyond* (Totowa, N.J.: Rowman and Littlefield, 1983).

Leszek Kolakowski, *Main Currents of Marxism,* vol. 3 (Oxford: Oxford University Press, 1978).

Alasdair MacIntyre, *Herbert Marcuse* (New York: Viking Press, 1970).

Herbert Marcuse, *Reason and Revolution: Hegel and the Rise of Social Theory* (New York: Oxford University Press, 1941).

Robert W. Marks, *The Meaning of Marcuse* (New York: Ballantine Books, 1970).

Ronald Nash, *Freedom, Justice and the State* (Lanham, Md.: University Press of America, 1980).

Ronald Nash, *Poverty and Wealth* (Richardson, Tex.: Probe Books, 1992).

Ronald Nash, *Why the Left Is Not Right: The Religious Left: Who They Are and What They Believe* (Grand Rapids: Zondervan, 1996).

Robert Tucker, *Philosophy and Myth in Karl Marx* (Cambridge: Harvard University Press, 1961).

Eliseo Vivas, *Contra Marcuse* (New York: Delta, 1971).

NOTES

Chapter One

1. Gordon Graham, *The Shape of the Past* (New York: Oxford University Press, 1997), 2.

2. Ibid.

3. Spanning the time roughly from 1750 to 1950, the term "philosophy of history" was a common name for the speculative approach to history. In the last fifty years or so, the connotation of the term has been greatly expanded so that it also includes questions about how scientific historians do their work: of understanding and explaining the past. For most of this book, I will use "philosophy of history" in the older and more narrow sense. For more background on this, see Ronald Nash, *Christian Faith and Historical Understanding* (Richardson, Tex.: Probe, 1992), chap. 1.

4. Contemporary students of history have come to see that scientific historians must deal with more than individual facts. For more on this subject, see Nash, ibid., chap. 3.

5. With regard to these questions, I follow the lead of William H. Dray in his book *Philosophy of History* (Englewood Cliffs, N.J.: Prentice-Hall, 1964), 63ff.

6. John P. Newport, *Life's Ultimate Questions* (Dallas: Word, 1979), 40.

7. No scientific historian is ever as detached as some suggest. See Nash, *Christian Faith and Historical Understanding*, chaps. 5–6.

8. Herbert Butterfield, *Christianity and History* (London: Bell, 1949), 3.

9. Ibid., 119.

10. The sense of "proof" in this context is a subject of some debate. See Ronald Nash, *Faith and Reason* (Grand Rapids: Zondervan, 1988), chap. 4.

11. T. A. Roberts, *History and Christian Apologetics* (London: SPCK, 1960), vii.

12. See Acts 9:1–31.

13. Gordon H. Clark, *A Christian View of Men and Things* (Unicoi, Tenn.: The Trinity Foundation, 1991), 80–81.

14. Christopher Dawson, *Dynamics of World History*, ed. John J. Mulloy (LaSalle, Ill.: Sherwood Sugden & Co., 1978), 251.

15. J. Gresham Machen, *What Is Christianity?* (Grand Rapids: Eerdmans, 1951), 18.

16. Ibid.

17. For examples, see Ronald Nash, *Great Divides* (Colorado Springs: Nav-Press, 1993), chap. 3.

Chapter Two

1. For more detail about the debate between Christian theism and panentheism, see Ronald Nash, *The Concept of God* (Grand Rapids: Zondervan, 1984), and Ronald Nash, ed., *Process Theology* (Grand Rapids: Baker, 1987).

2. For an analysis of many of the philosophical issues that arise in connection with such attributes, see Ronald Nash, *The Concept of God.*

3. For a criticism of some recent attacks on the deity and humanity of Jesus, see Ronald Nash, *Is Jesus the Only Savior?* (Grand Rapids: Zondervan, 1994).

4. The doctrine of creation *ex nihilo* teaches that there was no preexisting stuff from which God made the world. Before God created, there was nothing but God.

5. The adjective is crucial here since over the centuries many thinkers have applied the word *Christian* to very different, in fact opposing, worldviews.

6. Attacks upon this claim have become a staple of heterodox thinking within the church. But the rejection of this kind of propositional revelation is seldom supported by arguments. See Ronald Nash, *The Word of God and the Mind of Man* (Phillipsburg, N.J.: Presbyterian and Reformed, 1992).

7. I explore many of these issues in books such as Ronald Nash, *The Word of God and the Mind of Man*, already cited, and Ronald Nash, *Faith and Reason* (Grand Rapids: Zondervan, 1988).

8. See chap. 3 of Nash, *Faith and Reason.*

9. For more detail about these worldviews, see Ronald Nash, *The Gospel and the Greeks* (Richardson, Tex.: Probe, 1992), Part Two.

10. The past tense is advisable in this sentence because Western culture is being invaded by such systems as Islam and religious worldviews from the Orient which in some cases have mutated into what has come to be known as New Age thinking.

11. The word "metaphysical" helps distinguish the type of naturalism I am discussing from other varieties, such as Ethical Naturalism.

12. William H. Halverson, *A Concise Introduction to Philosophy*, 3rd ed. (New York: Random House, 1976), 394.

13. Ibid.

14. Some naturalists attempt to argue that the theist's understanding of reality alters the foundations of science so radically as to, in effect, make it impossible. Interested readers will find a rebuttal to this point in several sources including Ronald Nash, *Faith and Reason*, chap. 17; Jerry Gill, *Faith in Dialogue* (Waco, Tex.: Word, 1985), 33ff; and Richard Bube, *The Human Quest* (Waco, Tex.: Word, 1971), 115ff.

15. This touches on another complex issue that I do not have time to pursue in this book, namely, whether miracles must be viewed as violations of the laws of nature. In another book, I counsel against this position, although I recognize that many other Christian theists define miracles as exceptions to the laws of nature. See Ronald Nash, *Faith and Reason*, chaps. 16–17.

16. I discuss the criteria by which we should test worldviews in my books, *Worldviews in Conflict* (Grand Rapids: Zondervan, 1992) and *Faith and Reason* (already cited). The tests include reason or logical consistency, outer experience (conformity to what we know about the world around us), inner experience (conformity to what we know about our own nature), and the claim that any worldview worthy of our respect ought to be a system we can live out in our everyday life.

17. C. S. Lewis, *Miracles* (New York: Macmillan, 1960), 12. I am following his argument in the second edition of the book. The first edition contained an argument against naturalism that Lewis came to see as fallacious.

18. Ibid., 14.

19. Ibid., 14–15.

20. The kind of argument Lewis rejects here is similar to the fallacious argument he himself had advanced (and later rejected) in the first edition of *Miracles.*

21. For example, a person suffering from a particular disorder might believe something because he "hears" an inner voice. We tend to judge such people as mad when their conclusions lack any justifying ground. The beliefs of the philosopher I describe may also have a cause, for example, something that happened in the philosopher's childhood perhaps. One would hope that a person aspiring to the title of philosopher would be able to produce grounds for his beliefs.

22. Lewis, *Miracles*, 16.

23. Ibid., 18.

24. Richard L. Purtill, *Reason to Believe* (Grand Rapids: Eerdmans, 1974), 44.

25. While my earlier remarks did not discuss ethics, moral principles seem to be in as much difficulty in the worldview of metaphysical naturalists as logical principles. Treating both adequately certainly seems to force us to recognize the existence of things that transcend the purely natural order, that exist, in other words, outside of the box.

26. For more detail, see Herman Dooyeweerd, *In the Twilight of Western Thought* (Philadelphia: Presbyterian and Reformed, 1960) and Ronald Nash, *Dooyeweerd and the Amsterdam Philosophy* (Grand Rapids: Zondervan, 1962), chap. 7.

27. Henry Zylstra, *Testament of Vision* (Grand Rapids: Eerdmans, 1958), 145.

Chapter Three

1. See Grace Cairns, *Philosophies of History* (London: Peter Owen, 1963).

2. J. B. Bury, *The Idea of Progress* (New York: Macmillan, 1932), 12.

3. See John Baillie, *The Belief in Progress* (New York: Charles Scribner's Sons, 1951), 44–45.

4. Bury, op. cit., 12.

5. Ibid.

6. John Warwick Montgomery, *The Shape of the Past: An Introduction to Philosophical Historiography* (Ann Arbor, Mich.: Edwards Bros., 1962), 42.

7. For a refutation of the claim that the Stoic doctrine of universal conflagration influenced any New Testament writers, see Ronald Nash, *The Gospel and the Greeks* (Richardson, Tex.: Probe, 1992), chap. 4.

8. The philosophers of the Middle Stoa replaced the doctrine of universal conflagration with a belief in the eternity of the world.

9. Baillie, *The Belief in Progress,* 48.

10. Marcus Aurelius Antoninus, *Meditations*, 11/1, trans. Maxwell Staniforth (London: Hammondsworth, 1964), 165.

11. British scholar John Baillie is but one example. See Baillie's *The Belief in Progress*, 55–56.

12. Introductory Comments to the Book of Ecclesiastes, no credited author, *New Geneva Study Bible*, Luder Whitlock, Executive Editor (Nashville: Thomas Nelson Publishers, 1995), 986.

13. For a short analysis of both, see Ronald Nash, *The Closing of the American Heart* (Richardson, Tex.: Probe, 1990), 70–74.

14. Frederick Nietzsche, *The Gay Science,* #341, tr. I. Reinhardt in *Nietzsche's Collected Works,* ed. O. Levy (New York, 1909), 270–71. This work is sometimes published under the title *The Joyful Wisdom.*

15. See Ronald Nash, *Worldviews in Conflict* (Grand Rapids: Zondervan, 1992), chap. 8.

16. Gordon H. Clark, *A Christian View of Men and Things* (Unicoi, Tenn.: The Trinity Foundation, 1991), 77.

17. Ibid., 78.

Chapter Four

1. The dates for Origen, Tertullian, and Justin Martyr are as close as we can get.

2. See Amos 6:14; 9:8–9.

3. The word *hellenistic* is given to the period of history that began with the death of Alexander the Great in 323 B.C. and ended with the Roman conquest in 30 B.C. of the last major vestige of Alexander's empire, the Egypt of Cleopatra. Eventually, the term came to be applied to the culture of the Roman Empire as well. While Rome achieved military and political supremacy throughout the Mediterranean world, it adopted the culture of the Hellenistic world that preceded its rise to power.

4. *Hellenistic Judaism* is the official term for the beliefs and customs of Jews who adopted the Greek language and the philosophy and thinking of their Hellenis-

tic culture. *Alexandrian Judaism* is, quite obviously, a label for Hellenistic Jews who submitted to Hellenistic influences because of their contact with the Jewish community in Alexandria, Egypt.

5. John 1:1 says, "In the beginning was the Word (Logos) and the Word (Logos) was with God and the Word (Logos) was God.

6. See Ronald Nash, *The Gospel and the Greeks* (Richardson, Tx: Probe Books, 1992), chaps. 5–6.

7. See Philo's *Allegorical Interpretation* 3, 25; *On the Creation* 60. For more on this subject, see Ronald Williamson, *Philo and the Epistle to the Hebrews* (Leiden: E. J. Brill, 1970), 148ff. For a recently published edition of Philo's writings, see *The Works of Philo*, tr. C. D. Yonge (Peabody, Mass.: Hendrickson, 1993).

8. From a number of passages in Hebrews, it is possible to doubt the genuineness of the commitment made by some members of this community, as witnessed by Hebrews 6:1–12. None of the expressions applied to the recipients of the letter in these verses necessarily describe people who have had a genuine conversion experience.

9. Ronald Williamson cites most of the important sources on both sides of the question in the first chapter of his *Philo and the Epistle to the Hebrews,* already cited. Even though Williamson acknowledges the familiarity of the author with Alexandrian Judaism, he is skeptical when it comes to the matter of a personal acquaintance with Philo's philosophy. Contemporary evangelicals like F. F. Bruce have pointed out the apparent familiarity of the writer of Hebrews with some teachings of Philo. See F. F. Bruce, *The Epistle to the Hebrews* (Grand Rapids: Eerdmans, 1964), lxix and following, as well as Bruce's commentary on Hebrews in Peake's *Commentary on the Bible*, ed. M. Black and H. H. Rowley, rev. ed. (New York: Nelson, 1962), 1008.

10. There are two diametrically opposing views concerning the relationship between the book of Hebrews and the thought of Philo and Alexandrian Judaism. The one extreme, typified by French scholar C. Spicq, holds that the author of Hebrews was definitely influenced in a direct manner by the writings of Philo. The writer may have known Philo personally; he certainly read some of his writings; he may have been a convert from Alexandrian Judaism to Christianity. More moderate versions of this thesis have for years found expression in the literature about Hebrews. Spicq's commentary on Hebrews remains one of the most detailed and fully documented works arguing for a strong and direct Philonic influence on Hebrews. In 1970, however, Ronald Williamson challenged Spicq's contentions. Williamson successfully pointed out a number of weaknesses in Spicq's case. Although Williamson strayed too far in the opposite direction in his effort to rule out any Philonic influence, he was correct in claiming that interpreters have tended to exaggerate Philo's influence on the book of Hebrews.

11. See Nash, *The Gospel and the Greeks,* chap. 6.

12. Hebrews 7:27, NIV, author's emphasis.

13. Hebrews 9:25–28, NIV.

14. Williamson, *Philo and the Epistle to the Hebrews*, 148.

15. *Cephas* is the Greek equivalent of Peter.

Chapter Five

1. See Ronald Nash, *The Light of the Mind: St. Augustine's Theory of Knowledge* (Lexington, Ky.: University Press of Kentucky, 1969).

2. Augustine, *The City of God*, tr. Marcus Dodd (Edinburgh: T & T Clark, 1881), 14, 28, pp. 282–83. In succeeding references to this work, the first number is the book while the second is the chapter.

3. Ibid., 15, 1, p. 285.

4. This is the central message of *Revelation*, chap.12.

5. Augustine, *The City of God,* 14, 28, p. 283.

6. John Edward Sullivan, *Prophets of the West* (New York: Holt, Rinehart and Winston, 1970), 4.

7. Augustine, *The City of God,* 5, 1, p. 84.

8. See *Revelation*, chaps. 20–22.

9. Augustine, *The City of God*, 12, 13, p. 234.

10. Ibid.

11. Ibid.

12. Some recent approaches to Augustine's thought have gone much too far in claiming his dependence upon the Neo-platonic philosophy of Plotinus. It is true that Augustine's discovery of Plotinus helped remove some of the final obstacles standing between him and his Christian conversion. This was especially true in the case of the problem of evil. It is also true that important elements of Augustine's philosophical system bear evidence of Plotinus's influence. But on every essential issue where an irreconcilable clash between Augustine's Christian faith and Neoplatonism arises, the mature Augustine never hesitates to repudiate Plotinus's doctrine.

13. Gordon H. Clark, *A Christian View of Men and Things* (Unicoi, Tenn.: The Trinity Foundation, 1991), 85. I am indebted to Dr. Clark for these four points.

14. Augustine, *The City of God*, 14, 28, p. 86.

15. Clark, *A Christian View of Men and Things*, 88.

16. Augustine, *The City of God*, 19, 4, p. 401.

17. Ibid., 19, 27, pp. 419–20.

18. See Augustine, *The City of God*, 19, 5, pp. 403–404.

19. Ibid., 9, 10, p. 406.

20. Ibid., 19, 13, p. 409.

21. A worthwhile exercise at this point would be a careful reading of the New Testament passages that speak of the war going on within each human being. See Romans 7:21–25; Galatians 5:16–17; James 4:1; and 1 Peter 2:1.

22. See, for example, Romans 5:10.

23. Ephesians 2:17.

24. Colossians 1:20.

25. Romans 5:1–2.

26. Augustine, *The City of God,* 22, 30, p. 511.

Chapter Six

1. See Ronald H. Nash, *Christian Faith and Historical Understanding* (Grand Rapids, Mich.: Zondervan, 1984), chap. 3.

2. See René Descartes, *A Discourse on Method*, Part One.

3. The expression combines the Latin words for "truth" and "made," conveying the idea that one can know something best when one has made it.

4. *The New Science of Giambattista Vico*, tr. Thomas Goddard Bergin and Max Harold Fisch, rev. ed. (Ithaca, N.Y.: Cornell University Press, 1968), section 331, p. 96.

5. Alan Donagan, *Philosophy of History* (New York: Macmillan, 1965), 7.

6. For more about this point, see chapter 3 of Ronald Nash, *Christian Faith and Historical Understanding.*

7. 1725, 1730, and 1744. My quotations come from the 1744 edition in the Bergin-Fisch translation.

8. Note Vico's emphasis upon human progress.

9. The expansion from the order of the family to the larger communities of the city, nation, and species.

10. *The New Science of Giambattista Vico*, section 341, pp. 101–102.

11. Ibid., section 178, p. 70.

12. Pardon E. Tillinghast, *Approaches to History* (Englewood Cliffs, N.J.: Prentice-Hall, 1963), 124.

Chapter Seven

1. See Ronald Nash, *The Word of God and the Mind of Man* (Phillipsburg, N.J.: Presbyterian and Reformed, 1992), chap. 2.

2. These essays along with a helpful introduction by the editor are published in *On History*, by Immanuel Kant, ed. Lewis White Beck (New York: Bobbs-Merrill, 1963).

3. Immanuel Kant, "Idea of a Universal History From a Cosmopolitan Point of View," Proposition Eight. I use the W. Hastie translation published in London in 1914. The entire essay has been reprinted in *Theories of History*, ed. Patrick Gardiner (New York: Free Press, 1959). The quote appears on p. 30.

4. Introduction to Kant's "Idea of Universal History," in Gardiner, 23.

5. Ibid.

6. Proposition Four, Gardiner, 25.

7. Individualism is often maligned by people who fail to distinguish diverse senses of the word. In addition to the selfish individualism mentioned above, a more important type of individualism is simply a defense of the rights of individual persons against totalitarian or quasi-totalitarian governments. In this second sense, individualism is the opposite of statism. See Ronald Nash, *Freedom, Justice and the State* (Lanham, Md.: University Press of America, 1980).

8. The similarity of Kant's position to Vico's doctrine of providence should be noted. It should also be compared with Hegel's concept of the "cunning of reason."

9. F. L. Cross and Elizabeth A. Livingstone, eds., *The Oxford Dictionary of the Christian Church* (London: Oxford University Press, 1974), 104.

10. Many professing Christians make this blunder. I criticize them in several of my books, such as *The Word of God and the Mind of Man* and *Worldviews in Conflict* (Grand Rapids: Zondervan, 1992).

11. The word *supernatural* here has absolutely nothing to do with Hollywood movies and horror novels. It is used instead to name the belief that nature, the realm of natural occurrences, is not all there is to reality. Indeed, there is a reality above nature, and since that reality includes the Creator God of the Christian faith, the natural order that is everything for the naturalist would never have existed with the supernatural God who created the natural order.

12. George P. Grant, *Philosophy in the Mass Age* (Vancouver: Copp Clark, 1959), 49.

13. D. W. Bebbington, *Patterns of History* (Downers Grove, Ill.: InterVarsity Press, 1979), 68.

14. Charles Darwin, *The Origin of Species* (London: 1897), 402.

15. Benjamin Wirt Farley, *The Providence of God* (Grand Rapids: Baker, 1988), 193.

16. Harold O. J. Brown, *Heresies* (Garden City, N.Y.: Doubleday, 1984), 417.

17. I discuss historicism in the next chapter.

18. Bebbington, *Patterns of History*, 91.

19. John P. Newport, *Life's Ultimate Questions* (Dallas: Word, 1989), 60.

20. Ibid.

21. Carl F. H. Henry, *The Remaking of the Modern Mind*, 2d ed. (Grand Rapids: Eerdmans, 1948), 43.

22. Ibid., 43–44.

23. This point is so famous, it even has a name: *modus tollens.*

24. Gordon H. Clark, *A Christian View of Men and Things* (Unicoi, Tenn.: The Trinity Foundation, 1991), 46.

25. Some of the material in this section is adapted from Gordon Clark's discussion of progress in his book *A Christian View of Men and Things.*

26. In this case, if B . . .

27. Then C.

28. J. B. Bury, *The Idea of Progress* (New York: Macmillan, 1932), 351–52.

29. Ibid., 352.

30. Clark, *A Christian View of Men and Things*, 53.

31. This point is relevant since all proponents of the progress dogma talk about human free will. What we have here is a logical contradiction located at the very heart of the progress theory.

32. Important differences exist between the type of impersonal fatalism that is entailed by the doctrine of progress and the view of the Reformed faith that goals and ends predetermined by God are inseparable from the means leading to those ends, among which are included significant human choices.

33. This introduces still another test by which we should evaluate worldviews, the test of outer experience. Does our worldview fit naturally and comfortably with what we know about the world outside of us?

Chapter Eight

1. Johann Gottfriend Herder, *Outlines of a Philosophy of the History of Man.* My quotations come from the second edition of T. O. Churchill's English translation published in London in 1804. Because sections of this translation have been published many times using different pagination, I locate my quotes by the title of the section rather than page number. This quote appears in the Introduction to Herder's book.

2. Herder, "The Principal Law of History."

3. Ibid.

4. Herder, "General Reflections on the History of Greece."

5. Pardon E. Tillinghast, *Approaches to History* (Englewood Cliffs, N.J.: Prentice-Hall, 1963), 150.

6. There is a second sense of "historicism" that deals with discovering the pattern of the past and on that basis predicting the future.

7. D. W. Bebbington, *Patterns of History* (Downers Grove, Ill.: InterVarsity Press, 1979), 93–94.

8. See Bebbington, *Patterns in History*, 114.

Chapter Nine

1. R. G. Collingwood, *The Idea of History* (New York: Oxford University Press, 1946), 113.

2. R. S. Hartman in the introduction to his translation of Hegel's Introduction to his *Lectures*, published under the title *Reason in History* (New York: Liberal Arts Press, 1953), ix. Hartman is referring, of course, to Hegel's impact on history through his influence on Communism and Fascism. The history of this influence is traced in Sidney Hook's *From Hegel to Marx* (Ann Arbor, Mich.: University of Michigan Press, 1962).

3. Jon Stewart, "Introduction," in *The Hegel Myths and Legends,* ed. Jon Stewart (Evanston, Ill.: Northwestern University Press, 1996), 2.

4. Robert Heiss, *Hegel, Kierkegaard, Marx*, tr. by E. G. Garside (New York: Delta, 1975).

5. Burleigh Taylor Wilkins, *Hegel's Philosophy of History* (Ithaca, N.Y.: Cornell University Press, 1974), 56–57.

6. Samuel Enoch Stumpf, *Socrates to Sartre,* 4th ed. (New York: McGraw-Hill, 1966), 329.

7. Jon Stewart, ed., *The Hegel Myths and Legends* (Evanston, Ill.: Northwestern University Press, 1996), from the editor's introduction.

8. To cite just two examples, see the respected history of philosophy text, *Socrates to Sartre* by Samuel Enoch Stumpf, 4th ed. (New York: McGraw-Hill, 1966), 330–31, as well as John P. Newport, *Life's Ultimate Questions* (Dallas: Word, 1989), 58.

9. Gustav E. Mueller, "The Hegel Legend of 'Thesis-Antithesis-Synthesis,'" in *Journal of the History of Ideas*, Vol. 19 (1958), 411–14.

10. Ibid., 412. For the full context, see G. W. F. Hegel, *Phenomenology of Spirit*, tr. A. V. Miller (New York: Oxford University Press, 1979), Section #50 of the Preface, p. 29.

11. See Mueller's account on 413–14.

12. Ibid., 413.

13. Ibid., 414.

14. Walter Kaufmann, *Hegel: A Reinterpretation* (New York: Doubleday, 1965), 154.

15. Ibid.

16. Ibid., 155.

17. Ibid., 198.

18. Ibid., 203.

19. This is tricky for inattentive readers. The physical universe demonstrates no progress while human beings do show movement towards a goal.

20. *Holism* in this sense is an approach to human beings and their institutions that rejects the primacy of individual persons and places its emphasis instead on the larger groups of which humans are a part.

21. *Statism* is a political ideology that elevates government (the state) above individual persons. To extend footnote 20, the state takes precedence in Hegel's thinking over not only individuals but also over other groups such as the family and voluntary social groups such as churches.

22. Georg Wilhelm Friedrich Hegel, *The Philosophy of History*, tr. J. Sibree (New York: Dover Publications, 1956), 39.

23. Ibid.

24. I use here the translation by R. S. Hartman in his edited version of Hegel's Introduction to his lectures, published under the title of *Reason in History* (New York: Library of Liberal Arts, 1953), 27.

25. See Hartman edition, 44.

26. Hegel, Dover edition, 31.

27. I use the male personal pronoun here because Hegel does.

28. Once again, I use male nouns and pronouns because Hegel does.

29. Another comment about Hegel's obscure language is necessary. *Universal man* is humankind in its holistic dimension, under the law as part of the State. The opposite of this is the belief that individual men and women can be free, regardless of their relationship to the larger group.

Chapter Ten

1. Paul Johnson, *Intellectuals* (New York: Harper and Row, 1988), 67–68.

2. Any naturalist who is not an ethical relativist is obliged to tell us the source of his non-relativistic ethical principles and give the reasons why we should care about his moral opinions.

3. Sidney Hook, *From Hegel to Marx* (Ann Arbor: University of Michigan Press, 1962), 15–16.

4. From the preface to Karl Marx's *A Contribution to the Critique of Political Economy*, trans. N. I. Stone (Chicago: Charles H. Kerr and Co., 1904).

5. Sidney Hook, *Marx and the Marxists: The Ambiguous Legacy* (Princeton: Van Nostrand, 1955), 19.

6. D. W. Bebbington, *Patterns in History* (Downers Grove, Ill.: InterVarsity Press, 1979), 138.

7. See Engels's letter to J. Block, 21–22 of September 1890, contained in Engels *Selected Works*, vol. 2, p. 443.

8. Marx, of course, did not think his understanding of the dialectic was a myth. He believed the myth was true.

9. V. I. Lenin, *Teachings of Karl Marx* (New York: International Publishers, 1930), 17.

10. Marx and Engels, *The Manifesto of the Communist Party* by Karl Marx and Friedrich Engels, authorized English translation, ed. Engels (Chicago: Charles H. Kerr and Co., 1888), Section I, *Bourgeois and Proletarians.*

11. After Marx's death, Engels alligned himself with this position.

12. Marx, preface to *A Contribution to the Critique of Political Economy.*

13. E. H. Carr, *Studies in Revolution* (London: Macmillan, 1950), 24–25.

14. For a detailed account of these blunders, see Paul Johnson, *Modern Times* (New York: Harper and Row, 1983), chap. 2.

15. Sidney Hook, *Marx and the Marxists*, 35.

16. Ibid., 36.

17. Ibid., 37.

18. Ibid., 38.

19. Ibid., 39.

20. This is a reference to Marx's famous statement that in the classless society, the basic principle of distribution will be "from each according to his ability to each according to his need."

21. Ibid., 44–45.

22. Ibid., 45.

23. See Ronald Nash, *Poverty and Wealth: Why Socialism Doesn't Work* (Richardson, Tex.: Probe Books, 1992).

24. Alan Besancon, "Forgotten Communism," *Commentary* (January 1998), 24 [article appears on pp. 24–27].

25. Ibid., 24.

26. Ibid., 25.

27. John Frame, "Do We Need God to Be Moral?" *Free Inquiry*, (Spring 1996), 5–6. The article is a debate between Frame and Paul Kurtz and appears on pp. 4–7 of the issue.

28. Ibid., 6.

Chapter Eleven

1. Egyptian, Chinese, Ancient Semitic, Indian, Apollinian (Greek or Roman), Magian (Hebrew and Arabian), Faustian (or Western), and Mexican.

2. Gordon H. Clark, *A Christian View of Men and Things* (Unicoi, Tenn: The Trinity Foundation, 1991), 55.

3. Some critics have claimed that Spengler's position on this point helped prepare Germany for the advent of Adolf Hitler. Spengler supported Hitler when he assumed control of Germany in the early 1930s.

4. Volume 11, also published in 1961, was a historical atlas.

5. See chapter 1 of Toynbee's *Civilization on Trial* (Oxford: Oxford University Press, 1948) and *The Pattern of the Past* by Geyl, Toynbee, and Sorokin (Boston: Beacon Press, 1949), 73–94.

6. Toynbee uses the term the term *proletariat* to mean "any social element or group which in some way is 'in' but not 'of' any given society at any given stage of such society's history" (vol. 12, p. 306). Toynbee advises that there is no similarity between his use of the term and its appearance in Marx (vol. 12, p. 306). As representatives of a proletariat, Toynbee refers both to an Egyptian peasant and the relatively well-off slave of a powerful Roman magistrate. The term "includes anyone who is penalized in any respect—economically, politically, or socially. A person's material standard of living is not the criterion" (vol. 12, p. 306).

7. Arnold Toynbee, *A Study of History*, vol. 6 (London: Oxford University Press, 1939), 321.

8. See *A Study of History,* vol. 1, p. 51–64.

9. Vol. 6, p. 324.

10. Vol. 6, p. 326.

11. Vol. 7, pp. 154, 420.

12. Vol. 7, p. 423.

13. Arnold Toynbee, *A Study of History* (London: Oxford University Press, 1964), vol. 12, p. 519.

14. Ibid.

15. Ibid.

16. Volumes 7 through 10.

17. Christianity, Islam, Hinduism, and Buddhism.

18. Vol. 12, p. 307.

19. Vol. 12, p. 313.

20. For a detailed and critical analysis of various forms of religious pluralism like that espoused by Toynbee, see Ronald Nash, *Is Jesus the Only Savior?* (Grand Rapids: Zondervan, 1994).

21. Many of these criticisms can be found in books cited in the section "For Further Reading." Toynbee's vol. 12 presents an exhaustive account of such criticisms, along with his responses.

22. Christopher Dawson, *Dynamics of World History*, ed. John J. Mulloy (LaSalle, Ill.: Sherwood Sugden & Co., 1978), 392–93.

23. Ibid., 393.

24. Once again, for the many reasons why this sort of attempt can never work, see Nash, *Is Jesus the Only Savior?*

Chapter Twelve

1. See Humberto Belli and Ronald Nash, *Beyond Liberation Theology* (Grand Rapids: Baker, 1992).

2. See Ronald Nash, *Why the Left Is Not Right: The Religious Left: Who They Are and What They Believe* (Grand Rapids: Zondervan, 1996), chaps. 4, 9, and 10. See also Anthony Campolo, *We Have Met the Enemy and They Are Partly Right* (Waco, Tex.: Word, 1985), chaps. 7–9.

3. Tom Bottomore, *The Frankfurt School* (London: Routledge, 1989), 76.

4. For more on this, see Nash, *Why the Left Is Not Right,* chap. 3.

5. See Bottomore, *The Frankfurt School*, 12.

6. Robert W. Marks, *The Meaning of Marcuse* (New York: Ballantine Books, 1970).

7. These manuscripts, along with a helpful introduction, can be found in *Karl Marx: Early Writings*, tr. and ed. T. B. Bottomore (New York: McGraw-Hill, 1964).

8. For a description of Socialist alienation in Communist China, see *Time* magazine, November 28, 1983, p. 45. Among other things, the article notes that since 1978, Chinese journals have published six hundred articles on alienation. It is predictable that such alienation in a Socialist society will be blamed on spiritual pollution from the West.

9. Sidney Hook, *Marxism and Beyond* (Totowa, N.J.: Rowman and Littlefield, 1983), 46.

10. Daniel Bell, *The End of Ideology* (New York: Free Press, 1960), 344.

11. Hook, *Marxism and Beyond*, 46.

12. Erich Fromm, *Marx's Concept of Man* (New York: Ungar, 1961), 79.

13. Sidney Hook, "Marxism in the Western World," in *Marxist Ideology in the Contemporary World* (New York: Frederick A. Praeger, 1966), 16.

14. Ibid., 27.

15. Robert Tucker, *Philosophy and Myth in Karl Marx* (Cambridge: Harvard University Press, 1961), 235.

16. See Hook, *Marxism and Beyond*, 48; Daniel Bell, *The End of Ideology*, 394, along with Bell's "The 'Rediscovery' of Alienation," *The Journal of Philosophy*, vol. 56 (1959), 933–52.

17. See Belli and Nash, *Beyond Liberation Theology,* chap. 3.

18. Bottomore, *The Frankfurt School,* 39.

19. Herbert Marcuse, *One-Dimensional Man* (Boston: Beacon, 1964), Chap. 1.

20. Described in one of three essays by Herbert Marcuse, R. P. Wolff, and Barrington Moore, Jr., *A Critique of Pure Tolerance* (Boston: Beacon, 1967). Another source for many of Marcuse's ideas reported here is *An Essay on Liberation* (Boston: Beacon, 1969).

21. See Marcuse, Wolff, and Moore, *Critique of Pure Tolerance,* 87.

22. See Dale Vree, "A Comment on 'Some Irrational Sources of Opposition to the Market System,'" in *Capitalism: Sources of Hostility*, ed. Ernest van den Haag (New Rochelle, N.Y.: Epoch, 1979), 155–56.

23. It is important at this point not to allow followers of Marcuse to wriggle out of this predicament by claiming that he never intended his statements to apply to every person living under capitalism. His language makes clear this was his intention. Had Marcuse only said that *some* humans are totally preconditioned so that they cannot break free, his statement would have been true, but trivial; no one

denies it. For his claim to have any bite, he had to mean that *everyone* living in a capitalist society is caught in the trap. While this frees his claim from triviality, it creates the new predicament from which no one, not even Marcuse, can escape.

24. I support this statement in my book, *Why the Left Is Not Right*, already cited.

25. Lee Congdon, "The Marxist Chameleon," *The Intercollegiate Review*, 23 (fall 1987), 15.

26. Ibid.

27. See Bottomore, *The Frankfurt School,* 14. For a discussion of important parallels between the thought of Gramsci and the critical theory of the Frankfurt School, see Renate Holub, *Antonio Gramsci: Beyond Marxism and Postmodernism* (London: Routledge, 1992), 12. For the record, there is no evidence of any personal contact between Gramsci and members of the Frankfurt School (see Holub, 14). But Gramsci and the Germans were certainly traveling on parallel tracks.

28. See Antonio Gramsci, *Pre-Prison Writings*, ed. Richard Bellamy, tr. Virginia Cox (New York: Cambridge University Press, 1994) and chap. 11, "Antonio Gramsci" in *Marxism, Essential Writings*, ed. David McLellan (New York: Oxford University Press, 1988).

29. Congdon, p. 16.

30. Ibid.

31. Ibid., 17.

32. Ibid., 23.

33. See Benedetto Fontana, *Hegemony and Power* (Minneapolis: University of Minnesota Press, 1993), 140, 148–50.

34. Gordon H. Clark, *The Christian View of Men and Things* (Hobbs, N.M.: The Trinity Foundation, 1987), 93.

INDEX

C

D

E

F

G

H

J

K

L

M

N

O

P

R